The Mother God Returns

The Rise, Fall, and Recovery of the Feminine Divine

RENEE MCARDLE, PsyD

Copyright © 2020 Renee McArdle
All rights reserved.
ISBN: 979-8-89504-135-2

Published by Fair Andreen Incorporated
Waukesha, Wisconsin

DEDICATION

This book is dedicated to all of the women who kept and protected our truth and the the Rev. Frank S. Moyer, Lutheran Pastor, Hospital Chaplain and theological educator. He was a champion for women's rights, always lifting up Mother God in his prayers from the pulpit, marching for women's right to choose and challenging the religious structures to change the language and symbols which exclude women from the most sacred words of God.

CONTENTS

	Acknowledgments	i
	Introduction	1
1.	How We Internalize Symbols	11
2.	Meaning in People's Lives Is Revealed in the Stories They Tell	18
3.	My Story	24
4.	Making Words Matter	31
5.	No Longer Silent	38
6.	Reflections on the Women's Stories	84
7.	Call for Change	87
	Appendix & Bibliography	89
	About the Author	95

ACKNOWLEDGMENTS

There are many people I would like to thank. I am grateful for the significant women in my life, Cheryl McArdle, Carol Perrin, Therese Grumley, and Meg Larkin for their remarkable ability to be intuitive, honest, mysterious, and divine during this long process. I would also like to thank the members of my family. My mother, for encouraging me to love deeply, live outrageously, laugh shamelessly, and mother tenderly. My father for the constant easiness of his love, the respect and honor he gave women, the open mindedness he taught about all people and religions. My children, Allison, Bridgette, Jennifer, and Brian, whose laughter and emotional support was a respite from my task. The Rev. Frank S. Moyer, for his endless encouragement and and willingness to hold our life together, for without his sacrifice my dream would not have come to pass.

Courtney Oertel was the voice and wisdom as my personal editor, giving me the guidance to complete my life's call to write this book. I am forever grateful to her.

INTRODUCTION

Research psychologists who study the psychological development of men and women have asked themselves, "Why do women have more depression, lower self-esteem, and poorer self-concept than men?"

During my 25 years as a licensed clinical psychologist in Illinois, I started asking myself – and my peers – the same questions and came up with answers that went beyond the family of origin. No matter how good or bad their childhood experiences were, why did women internalize a self-identity that was less than men? I started looking deeper.

During my search for answers I found the work of Tony Wolfe, Jungian analyst and research scientist. Dr. Wolfe verified as early as 1934 from her research what I was experiencing with women today. Dr. Wolfe stated, "The psychological development of women has been significantly altered by the exclusive perception of God as Father. If the image of God is the supreme symbol of the highest human attributes and the most far reaching idea of the human spirit, then how can women find themselves if their own psychological principle and all its complexities are not objectified in a God symbol, as in the case for man?"

I continued to listen to hundreds of women's life stories and came to the same conclusion: there needs to be radical changes in the traditional theological and psychological Father God framework to include Mother God as an equal partner in the personhood of God, the Creator, so as to facilitate and enable an equal opportunity for women's psychological developmental success.

I discovered that masculine God language and imagery has communicated for centuries to women that they are nonentities, subspecies of men, subordinated and inferior to men not only on a religious but also on a cultural plane. Continuing my search, I found Joseph Campbell, an American professor of literature who worked in comparative mythology and comparative religion at Sarah Lawrence College. Campbell's research documents in *Myths to Live By* that the, "explicit relationship between belief in Father God and the societal practices" tells us nothing about God, but it does tell us much about how religion has defined our societal roles. So long as the prevailing male-centered definition and model of humanity seems adequate and accurate, there will be no change. This research conducted in 1972, remains relevant to the women of today.

As my research continued, I looked at the psychological development of women based on object relation theory, which is grounded in the research and study of the psychological development of both men and women on the internalization and identification of all societal symbols, which shapes one's identity. Because of the absence of a Mother God symbol operating in a girl's development, she has no female image of God to attach to, to identify with, or to internalize. This retards and limits the girl's achievement of optimal separation and individuation in forming herself and leads to an over idealization of men.

Western Christianity and Judaism are theistic in the view that God can be imaged as a person entering into a relationship of love and responsibility with humans. I am convinced that images of God as a male person without images of God as a female person dismiss the personhood of woman. In the same breath, I would like to say that I am quite aware that God is not really either female or male or anything in between. I am talking about the only thing we can talk about, words describing images of God, not God. WORDS MATTER. Still today, if it is daring and alienating to speak of God using female pronouns and imagery, then perhaps that indicates something about the way women and the feminine are valued. Therefore, we might say that the ultimate symbol of our demotion is our societies inability to say: "God-She."

God as Mother is breaking into the consciousness of women. Women are awakened to every place in society where they are not seen nor have a voice including the religious structures of hierarchy, where men sit at the top of the structure of power with dominance over what goes on in the religious institutions, political institutions, and in the workplace. As seen through social movements such as #MeToo, which began in 2018, crashing open the doors for women to psychologically break through their internal barriers of silence while gaining power over their own bodies.

What I recommend is a theory of development that recognizes the devastating wound to the psyche of women by the absence of the ultimate symbol of worth,

Mother God. I propose that no matter how hard feminist theorists work to bring value and power to what is feminine, until the ultimate value, God, is seen as feminine there will be low self-esteem for women and low esteem for women by others. I propose the answer lies in the relationship of the God symbol necessary in the early identity development of all children. The male child needs the Father God symbol, and the female child needs the Mother God symbol. While it sounds simple, changing any structure of power and dominance is very threatening to our society, as we know it.

Just imagine for a moment, the adolescent boy and adolescent girl step into the arena of the world, their bodies and minds are bursting into change – both are feeling excited and hopeful, ready to explore all the possibilities the world has to offer. The psychological and spiritual dimension in society is pivotal for development. They have given up their omnipotent appraisal of their mother and father for a more powerful mirror, now they are ready to have the world mirror for them through the image of God. To that extent, the boy and girl from this point forward have very different experiences.

The boy steps out waves to mom, looks and sees father and Father God beckoning him from the churches and synagogues and temples and on every coin in his pocket, from the invocations and prayers at community and sports events and national nominating conventions, from congregations across the world singing, "Faith of our Fathers" followed by the Creed. "We believe in one God the Father…" The lights turn up, the trumpets blow, and the boy walks through the door. The boy holds onto the male transitional Father God object with whom he identifies, reaffirming the omnipotence and power needed to maneuver his separation steps in the world.

The girl steps into the arena of the world also feeling the same excitement and hope, ready to explore all the possibilities the world has to offer. She waves to her father seeing Father God next to him, waves to mom and peers out the door. She sees nothing. No churches, no altars, no words, no steeples, no hymns, no creeds – wait a minute, what is this, a joke?

She waits and waits and waits. Finally abandoned by the ultimate feminine transitional object of the universe, she screams in agony, angry at her choices. Either, stay attached to mom or attach to father and the Father God. With those choices, the girl child cannot make the transition to personal autonomy and internal authority. object relations theory takes this story as one example of why women lose their core identity.

A client shared a story about her 10-year-old girl, upon leaving church after singing, "Peace on Earth, Good Will to Men" she asked, "Mom, doesn't God love women, too? Where is Mother God?" "Maybe Mother God is lost. Why couldn't she find me, I need her." Her mother said she continued to question. You know how children want their equal share.

Existential therapists, May and Yalom, (1989) in their research of women's excessive feeling of shame and guilt determined that they are experiences arising from failure to live up to one's potentialities. Potentialities are what a person is given in her/his origin, in the core of their being. In my private practice, shame and guilt is so prevalent in women's stories. Women feel shame and guilt when they choose themselves. Men experience guilt when they hurt someone else but when they tell stories where they choose themselves, they rarely express feeling shame or guilt. For women, without the internalization of the ultimate symbol of power, Mother God, as a gender confirmed act, their ultimate sense of worth gets distorted, confused, and lost.

Avery (1991) in her article about Gilligan's research with adolescent girls stated, "Girls are naturally assertive, with a vital sense of self. But the confidence is lost in the process of growing up." I propose this radical change occurs because the young girl has no omnipotent female God during her lifetime, thereby, the girl does not develop her naturally assertive, vital sense of self, into womanhood. Girl to Woman needs the energies of a Female God symbol, who carries the warrior and creator.

The problem I often address with my patients in their therapy sessions, is that women today continue to report more depression, more confusion, more guilt, lower self-esteem, a poorer self-concept, and more feelings of abandonment than men in a society that says women have political and economic equality. I ask women, "Aren't you tired of not getting served at the alter? Lady Justice is not the only one with a blindfold on." Sit in a church or temple and listen and feel deeply every time God, "the father," is used. Over and over scripture, hymns, confessions, creeds, again and again, kneel and bow to the masculine. There is no way to hold sacred the ultimate male symbol of God without men internalizing this supreme male image for themselves and excluding the female.

I ask women, "Aren't you tired of not having any word that refers to you held up as a sacred image in the most holy places?" It's in our churches, temples, schools, and on our flags! Even on money, you see "In God we Trust," every time you take a coin out of your pocket. We witness blessings at conferences, at the installation of our presidents, every time you place your hand on your heart and pledge allegiance to our country, "One Nation Under

God" – over and over and over – isn't 5,000 years of being ignored enough? Are we so used to being ignored that we stay silent?

Today, I sit and look out my window at the river moving slowly, carrying trees and leaves and other fallen beauty of nature and the truth slams into my gut. Why, I ask, does the word of GOD only carry a masculine image? It just doesn't make sense. Especially when I look at all of creation. Looking back at our history, during the Neolithic period, 7000–3500 BCE, archeologists have uncovered artifacts from a way of life that held Female as honored God. During this period, the temples honored the creation of humans coming out of the body of women. Every living creature was fed and nourished inside the woman whose body held the human tightly. She broke open and birthed the life – "here is my body broken for you." And, after the birth, her breasts, flowing with milk, she said, "take and eat, here is my body given for you" (Gimbutas, 1989).

This miracle of life was viewed with adoration, love and respect by both men and women. This miracle was seen in the energy of every blossom, every animal, and the earth itself bursting with life. They received the miracle of this life force and gave this experience the name GOD – Mother God, and both men and women felt this universal creation and co-created a partnership together with God Mother to bring the evolution of the world into fullness.

Nature was one with the Goddess. Earth, air, fire, and water were her symbols. Neolithic architecture was made of stone, emphasizing the centrality of the belief in the Goddesses. Archeologists found many large figures of the Mother Goddesses with large hips and breasts, arms held out, embracing the people. During this period 6000

BCE, on Crete, archeologists uncovered highly developed civilizations with palaces, villas, farmsteads, harbors, road networks, organized places of worship, and planned burial sites. Mother God was central, living the partnership between men and women.

As always where there is light, there is darkness. And the darkness came in 3000 BCE changing the world and the word, Mother God. The darkness came charging and killing with the metals which had been used to make beautiful alters and symbols of the Great Mother God into weapons of mass destruction, killing the men, raping and enslaving the women and children, and changing the God symbol from the loving creator Mother God to the Warrior Father God. The great temple of the Divine Mother was our foundation. Men and Women have been stripped of all primary representations of the Divine Mother, The Awesome She – God She.

Lost were the symbols, the words and the voices that prayed and sang to Mother God. No longer did women grow up seeing her face and God as one – her body and God as one. Every person becomes that which they see, hear, and which they identify with and internalize. Women lost the psychological process of internalizing the greatest power of all, God.

God – She created the world

God – She forgives all our sins

God – She is most wise

God – She is all-powerful

Women lost their identity while men continue, to this day, to identify with the most powerful symbol of all – God, the Father.

Two thousand years of Our Father, which art in Heaven – hallowed be thy name

Thy kingdom come, Thy will be done, On Earth as it is in Heaven.

Just replace Our Father with ALL MEN – hallowed be thy names,

Thy kingdom come, Thy will be done, On Earth as it is in Heaven.

We are talking Power – Domination – Honor – not God.

Too many people will say it doesn't matter – God is neither male nor female – God is the wind, the tree, the flame, and the mountain. Too many people will say it doesn't matter. I say it matters. Women can't make the leap to the wind, the flame, the tree, the mountain without first seeing the face of God as She. Men can, they take their male God with them into the flame, the wind, the mountain, the tree, the power, the glory on Earth as it is in Heaven. The universe needs to hold the female and male images equally. Women must demand the honor, the glory, and the "will be HERS on Earth as it is in Heaven."

Psychological scientific research has proven that it is not possible to erase an internalized image, experience, or memory without an over-lay: a new image, a new experience, or a new sound. When the new is internalized and identified with, then we are healed. When the new is born, the self-identity, the self-esteem – is born.

Men and women are needed to collaborate in a conscious awakening to create the partnership of Mother God–Father God and in turn, this will heal the wounds created by the exclusion of women from the word God.

1. HOW WE INTERNALIZE SYMBOLS

Object relations theory

As my research continued, I decided that object relations theory held the most promising study for the psychological development of all humans. This psychological developmental theory is based on the findings that all people internalize and identify with what they hear, see, feel – all that surrounds them. The following section describes object relations theory – as it relates to the origins of a personal representation of God to best explain why women, and men, must demand a change for the God symbol to include women.

According to McDargh (1983), object relations theory, a broad-based theoretical development within psychoanalysis, offers a way of understanding the, "origins of human religious sensibility, and in particular, the creation and elaboration of our images of the divine." The only large-scale clinical application of object relations theory to a problem central to the study of religion is Dr. Ana-Maria Rizzuto's 1979 research.

This contribution has linked the developmental origins of a God representation with what D.W. Winnicott (1971) identified as the human infant's capacity for the creation and use of transitional objects.

Rizzuto (1979) states:

In the contemporary western world God is spoken of most frequently as a person – a male person – a 'personal object' (p. 90), a father. Religion remains one of the most powerful regulatory structures of organized social life. If one religion disappears new systems of belief spring up to organize the meaning of the universe at large. The maturational ability to form a representation of God prepares a child to link themselves with cultural traditions and adapt to the type of culture in which she/he was born. The symbols/images powerfully mediate the spoken and unspoken sense of the individual regarding what is to be trusted and mistrusted, valued or avoided. Even for individuals who claim no explicit religious faith or whose faith has apparently moved beyond the mediation of a consciously held representation of God, it is uncanny says McCarthy (1983), "how often slips of the tongue, unexpected crises, or the candid telling of a life story will reveal the presence of a representation of God that was operative at one time in life and that seems to wait still in some not-quite-forgotten corner where it was left behind, exiled, banished or simply misplaced (p. 13).

Rizzuto (1979) concludes in her research: One of the most significant object representations with which an individual is in life-long relationship is the object representation of God. The factors which compound to form this representation are many and varied:

The pre-Oedipal psychic situation, the beginning state of the oedipal complex, the characteristics of the parents, the predicaments of the child with each of her/his parents and siblings, the general religious, social and intellectual background of the household, and even the unique circumstances in which the child may have been first introduced to the possibility of God by parents, neighbors or teachers (p. 45).

Once formed, that complex representation cannot be made to disappear; it can only be repressed, transformed, or used. The psychic process of creating and finding God – this personalized representational transitional object – never ceases in the course of human life. It is a developmental process that covers the entire life cycle from birth to death (Rizzuto, 1979). As in the individual, the same applies to historical development of humans from the dawn of creation to now.

Rizzuto's (1979) clinical research indicated that the child's and the adult's sense of self is affected by the representational traits of the individual's private God. Consciously, pre-consciously, or unconsciously, God, partly our own creation, like a piece of art, a painting, a melody, is reflecting what we have done, and affects our sense of ourselves. I propose that the child is profoundly affected by the imposed cultural God symbol, Father God, as well as the individual's private God.

Mirroring

One of the many ways a person develops a self-identity is through a psychological process called mirroring. It is the process of internalizing everything spoken and unspoken at an early age. The look and words of someone who loves us tells us we are loved, and we put it on the mirror within. The look and words of someone who tells us we are smart or stupid is internalized and shapes how we see ourselves also. We have a giant mirror within us which takes in everything and deeply influences our image of ourselves that we believe at a deep level and in turn shapes our capabilities to live our lives fully.

This mirroring process changes as new knowledge and new experiences are internalized and the old experiences have a deep influence if there are never new experiences to change them. For example, if we never hear the words Mother God presented next to Father God then we have no way of internalizing the most powerful image in the world spoken today. The most powerful symbol and authority is the God symbol. If we never have another God object to internalize to change our internal mirror, we as women will always have within us a male power as God. Thus, as woman we lack the very powerful object of psychology defining self-power, the ability to identify with Mother God to mirror for ourselves. Men have grown up from early childhood development with the God word meaning the highest power is masculine and so they look in the mirror and they are masculine, so they know they are as powerful as god.

Bringing the Female God into the Mirror

The following story confirms at least the possibility that a 3-year-old girl child may have female God images in her psyche. This story was told to me by a friend, she was reading the Christmas story to her granddaughter. Each time she would say that Mary gave birth to a boy, her granddaughter would explain loudly, "No, a GIRL!" "Mary had a girl." This went on throughout the whole story. Now the granddaughter's parents are not radical feminists, in fact, they are active members of a Methodist church. Somehow within this girl child is the natural conclusion that God is a female. I propose that it is more acceptable today for little girls to be able to speak her own truth.

All religions provide official or private rites of passage to facilitate the resolution of critical moments. Most of these dramatize the breaking of old bonds and the formation of new bonds between people. By making God or the Gods active participants in the process, ritual provides a new opportunity for the reshaping of the God representation and the individual's relation to it.

When I gave my retreats, they would be out and about from the hustle and bustle of life, someplace quiet and self-nurturing, requiring solitude and self-reflection. A time to journal and reflect on one's own life. The solitude of retreat allows one to be open to visualize the unknown.

My interest in solitude and retreat has been one of the main threads running through my life. A retreat is an act of nurturing the self. A women's retreat is about going within in order to listen and attune to your truest, most authentic self. It is to become self-restored. It is setting apart time to tend your inner life, feed your muse, reclaim your dreams. For me, I value the retreating, going-within cycle as much as accomplishing the out-in-the-world cycle.

In the evening, once we are in circle, we use music and guided imagery to help the participants enter into their inner world, to leave their outer world behind them for a time. One of my favorite guided visualizations begins with me asking the women to close their eyes and notice a road and see themselves walking down that road, to be aware of everything around them, on one side of the path they are on, they hear the sound of waves crashing to the shore. On the other side of the path they smell the pines and hear the birds. All the visualizations help center and bring each woman closer to her own path. Then they are told to walk slowly, toward a gate, their gaze sees beyond the gate, a door. The sun shines through the trees, the sounds of nature surround them, and they walk through the gate, toward the door and knock—and then She, Mother God, opens the door. The women are instructed to stay in silence, writing and feeling, internalizing this experience with the Divine-She.

The circle is formed once again, and it is here where women share their own experiences. Transformation and a new or renewed sense of her femininity and connection to the Divine are prevalent.

This is happening for women today. God, as Mother, is breaking into the consciousness of women. This transition is not only about inclusive language in all religious institutions, it is about all language referring to God, this is more profound and primary to a woman's self-hood. Women need today, as adults, the traditional God object that was not available to them as children, Mother God. The need for mirroring evolves and changes in the course of life but never ceases completely.

The sociocultural voices in the western world speak of God only as a male person, a father. The voices are not only the ministers, priests, rabbis – who represent Father God officially. God is totally established in this country as male, Father only. Most importantly, God is referred to as real, existing, powerful, and in charge of the world.

The Father God representation keeps in step with the personal identity transformation of the male and female self. The result of current psychological research studies indicated that all people in the western world form a God representation – one that may later be used, neglected, or actively repressed. In all cases the type of representation formed as a result of her/his personal experience will define her/his identity and her/his self-perception (Rizzuto, 1979). Importantly, Rizzuto's study reveals that both mother and father contribute their share. The entire representational process occurs in the wider context of the family, social class, organized religion, and particular subcultures.

Rizzuto concluded that Winnicott was accurate in locating religion – and God – in what is called the internalization of identity development transitional space. That is the place where a person's life finds the full relevance of her objects and meaning for herself. An early transitional god object needs to be female for the female child, so she develops physically and psychologically equal to men and his God image.

2. MEANING IN PEOPLE'S LIVES IS REVEALED IN THE STORIES THEY TELL

Meaning in people's lives is revealed in the stories they tell, and in their perceptions of forces with which they have to contend. Women need to regain faith in their own experiences and perceptions. They need to empower each other by telling their stories for others to hear and affirm. They need to grow in confidence in their own intuition. A male template has been placed over women's experience throughout history leaving women confused and depressed with heightened abandonment issues and lowered self-concept.

To study this need, I will be using qualitative research methods. Qualitative data provide depth and detail through direct quotation and careful description of individual units of analysis. Through the medium of personal stories, phenomenological techniques provide an understanding-descriptive method of analysis in place of the traditional and more common technological-experimental methodology. Such an approach assumes that experience is objectively real for self and others, existentially significant and, as such, can elucidate our understanding of women in their process of radical developmental change.

Women and men experience life differently, however, men have been articulating their experiences, written and verbal, and assuming them applicable to all. For a critique of the use of the male paradigm to formulate theory and research, I recommend reading, *Engendered Lives: A New Psychology of Women's Experience* by Ellyn Kaschak. Women have been forced to live out inauthentic stories, provided by a culture they did not create.

I wanted to find out more than just answering the question that self-esteem would be increased by identification with God who is female, and a female God would lessen confusion and a sense of abandonment. I wanted to listen to their process by which women in large numbers are turning to a worship of the Mother God.

What were the early signs from their bodies, from their dreams, from their relationships that heralded this radical event? What are the consequences, which such a subversive act, has made in their lives? And most important, in reflection, what have been the ramifications of not having a female god as girls growing up? These are process questions. This is process research.

One workshop I led was focused for Protestant women clergy who were in parishes from two to 10 years. The call to change the church structure to be inclusive to women was burning a hole in my soul. I wanted to know what these women ministers were doing.

My questions were: How have you brought feminist theology into education and worship experiences of your congregation? What is your relationship with your peers? What is the community that supports and inspires you, and what insights affect your ministry?

As I dialogued with them about women's issues in their church, they informed me that during training, the theological seminaries instruct and listen to women interns. These women felt affirmed during their time in seminary, that they could believe, at a deep level, their own spirituality. This would promote their need to change language to include the female, God – She in hymns, creeds, prayers, blessings, and the Godhead. They had support groups that created a sense of community enabling women seminarians to have the courage to face the world with radical action against oppressive institutions. But once the seminary doors close the women clergy are sprinkled sparsely throughout the religious communities. Isolated and alone, they are not able to continue the work the seminaries have started.

I knew three of the women previously mentioned but had little contact with them for several years since they first moved to the area. I was very surprised by their attitude when we connected again compared to when we met. One woman stated, "During Seminary training, we had access to support groups, but when we left Seminary we were out in 'A Man's World' and we had no support for us, as women, much less support for us as clergy, to change the structure." This was confirmed by the other clergywomen in our circle as well as our clergymen who were working toward this structure to include women and Mother God language – they were ignored.

One clergy woman who belongs to a progressive denomination which had published my official statement affirming a new feminist theology expressed her pain and anger when her own choir director refused to even discuss inclusive language in his hymn choices. REFUSES! She is the pastor and there is nowhere for her to go with her frustration. Her ecclesiastical government has little power to change the individual church communities. The support of her sisters is minimal because their numbers are minimal.

They all answered the first question similarly and I was totally depressed by their answers. They had tried in the beginning of their ministry, but they had no support from the male clergy toward any inclusive language and to survive these women became silent. They each had different ways of justifying their choices, but basically, they wanted to be "sensitive" to everyone. There is no way they can address the need for Mother God with Father God. They appeared unaware of their compromise. They no longer saw themselves or the women in their congregations as oppressed. They each expounded on the importance of being an individual, not associated with feminism or traditional patriarchy. "I try not to use any pronoun for God," was some of the most frequent statements. And the most troublesome was, "I've never used God – She even though I have prayed to Mother/Father God.

They explained that when they were with an all-female group the women in their congregation were threatened by a "woman minister doing what men always did" so they kept to the traditional. To my great distress, these wonderful, powerful, articulate women had not come to terms with their own pastoral identity as a woman in a man's place and they were tripping over it in their ministry to women. With all men's groups, they did not want to be insensitive to the men, therefore, they did not push for a new and inclusive theological awareness. These clergywomen began stuffing their knowledge and feelings the minute the seminary doors closed in order to survive, and with no close support from other clergywomen or men. They put their prophetic and liberating voice in the closet, and they put their spirit in a grey pinstripe suit.

Another clergywoman related the following incident, whereby, my eyes filled with tears at the violence done to her and the worst part is she no longer felt the pain. During one meeting of her ecclesiastical board, the president said while affirming her with these words: "She's a great guy."

The human being cannot live out of harmony with itself. Cognitive dissonance is a defense mechanism that allows one to survive in contradictory situations. If she wants a job, she must turn the other cheek and give "sensitive" care to her congregation and not confront the sexism. So, she keeps her prayers generic, her gray pinstriped suit pressed, overlooks sexist remarks and gives and gives and gives. I'm beginning to feel hopeless that transformation can work within the church.

What is the message for the highly trained professional clergywomen, who find themselves like the stump in the book, *The Giving Tree*, by Shel Silverstein. Giving, giving, she is literally exploited in the name of "sensitivity" to other's needs. In the story by Silverstein the tree is referred to as "she" and the little boy continually comes asking for parts of her, which she gladly gives seemingly with no needs of own self. Every church library has a copy and everyone "oos and aahs," exclaiming how wonderful to be so giving. My clergy sisters in the Protestant churches are dying. The patriarchal boy is sitting on her back and she doesn't yet know she is very angry. She is alone. She sees no others around her. When she turns and lift her eyes, all she sees are stumps, nothing but stumps, all with men sitting on them.

The seminaries provide the community, the prophetic word, the theological education, but it is not the real world. If she does get an appointment, there is no way she can take on the congregation alone. So, she becomes a champion for other causes. In order not to be forced to give up her call to ministry she uses her repressed anger to be a profound intellectual preacher, a compassionate zealot for peace and justice, a sensitive care-taker of her parishioners and with compromise as her crown, sensitivity as her wand, her back is bent over, and her heart is breaking.

My sister clergy are no longer pushing. They have no programs to educate congregations concerning feminist theology. They run into their parishioners who say they are tired of hearing about the errors of the past. They say, "be sensible, we just want to worship, we're all equal – what's the big issue, let's all sing together to show our support and love for one another." Now sing together, "Rise Up Oh Men of God."

The women clergy have stopped seeing themselves as victims of oppression; therefore, they do not feel anymore. They see themselves as the Great Mother. Breasts bare for all to suck. Legs spread to give birth to anyone who wants to crowd in or out. What they don't see is the Death Mother, teeth clenched, working in the shadows. Without the prophet, confronting the spirited voice of the Black Madonna to balance this passive unconsciousness of their ministry they will continue to be a stump for the patriarch to rest on as it grows old. She is the nanny caring for the children and cleaning the house of others, she is the Native American living in a square house while their spirit yearns to spin in a circle, she has gotten her pulpit but hasn't changed her song . . . "Rise Up Oh Men of God."

3. MY STORY

Before I asked the women in this study for their stories, I knew it was very important that they hear my story. As I reflected, I thought about my life experiences that were the platform from which I, with great passion, leapt off, into the conscious awareness – that my call in this lifetime was to bring the Great Mother God back to the top of the world power structure where She belongs, sitting with the Father God and sharing in the God symbol of creation and love. I shared the same challenges and frustrations as my fellow clergywomen and in order to answer this call, I knew it was time to leave my position in the church and begin working in private practice as a psychologist.

My spirituality was conceived in the womb of an attic in our home in Chicago where I slept with my grandmother and grandfather. I was 7 years old. After WWII, my dad came home from his tour of duty in Europe. He, my mother, my grandparents, my sister and I moved to South Chicago and bought a house together. My grandfather retired as a lieutenant in the Chicago Fire Department. During his time in the fire department, he inhaled a lot of smoke so he slept on one side of the attic next to the open window, so he could breathe the fresh air. My grandmother and I slept at the other window at the opposite side of the attic bedroom.

The "seeds" of my spiritual journey grew at the side of my bed where my grandmother and I would kneel each night in prayer. I remember kneeling with her, and her words still ring clearly in my ears: "Prayers are never to be said laying down. God is to be spoken to on your knees." "Yes Nana," I would reply while rubbing my aching knees. "Whatever do you say to God that takes so long," I asked. She replied, "It's the listening that takes the time, not the asking." She wove these words into our days together. She experienced a powerful union with God during her prayers, and that Wind blew around me as we knelt together.

My spiritual journey grew before I even realized it, as I would sit and hear our family tell the stories of Great Aunt Anne from Wales, and her healing powers and relationship to God. The mysteries of God were a reality for our family, but never in a legalistic way, as my family was also attached in many ways to the traditional churches: Catholic, Presbyterian, Episcopalian, and Spiritualist.

As I reflect back, still today, I have no recollection of entering the attic alone to sleep after her death. I was 10 years old when she died. A few months after her death, my mother said I went alone down to the Presbyterian church on the corner and joined the Sunday school. I went alone to church and I liked it. I experienced the most peace anywhere when I was in church listening to the sermons. I was glad to be alone with God. The church played a significant role in my spiritual development from that time on.

I grew up with wonderful stories of spirits and healing and miracles. While I was experiencing one type of spirituality with my grandmother, I had a different experience with my grandfather. He was injured battling the Chicago stockyards fire of 1912. He was told he would never be able to bend his knee again. During his recuperation time he began visiting his wife's sister, Aunt Anne, who was born in Wales and who was a known healer. During that year of weekly visits not only was my grandfather's knee healed, but he also learned about healing and found his own gift for healing. He met his spiritual Indian Guide, Siawa, and learned the chants and prayers of healing. People were always coming to our home and I would fall asleep to the sound of strange chants and mystery. I have a very strong spiritual base: the listening quiet prayer of my grandmother; the mysterious, powerful spiritual healing prayer of my grandfather, and the traditional church. This strong spiritual experience outside of the church allows me today to freely explore many avenues of spirituality without fear or guilt.

Even though my spiritual experience as a young child was balanced, my growing years after my grandparent's deaths were based on the teaching of the patriarchal church. This system had praise for me as leader and teacher, but no encouragement toward ordination.

I remember so well one Sunday; I was 15 and the pastor asked me to give the sermon and lead worship. After church I walked outside and started down the five steps to the sidewalk. I was "jolted" by a bright light streaming down from the sky, through the tallest tree, landing on my feet. I stopped dead in my tracks and looked up and followed the light from my feet, up through the tree and up into the sky. Just this year I was told by a woman, a nun who was secretly anointed into the priesthood of the

Catholic Church, "you know that was an anointing from God." I have never forgotten that moment, my anointment. In my meditation I go back to that moment and feel the heat on my feet from the light of God anointing me.

The greatest grief for me today, as I reflect back, is the vision of my call as minister never even got uttered from my lips. It stayed stuck in my heart until I was 37 years old. It enrages me yet, that I didn't even know I had a choice. Women were not called by any religious institute to be in the pulpit.

My call to be a minister when I was 15 years old was very strong. Clear as when I first heard the words 26 years ago. But where or what was my structure? I was plagued by my traditional side, which says, to be a minister one must be ordained. One part of myself wanted the blessing of the collective, wanted to be acknowledged as a minister by the patriarch. I wanted to wear the collar, mumble the Words, and walk with the Elders.

So, I struggled with my foundation – the mystical that is God, Grandmother, Mother, Female, and the traditional All Father, All Male.

I have always identified with God-She. When I was a hospital chaplain, I would pray with patients using Mother Father God. It got to when I entered the emergency room, the doctors on duty would say, "Mother is here" just as they would say, "Father is here" when a male minister or a priest came.

Finally, I followed my call to bring the Mother God to the world and entered McCormick Presbyterian Seminary in Chicago, thinking, "here is where change can happen." Women are being ignored at the most powerful sacred places – our prayers, our altars, our churches and temples throughout the world.

At the seminary and churches I served, I tried to bring awareness and change. I challenged the necessity of inclusive language. I taught and created new forms of worship. I was not accepted. I was ignored.

Outside the traditional system I flourished. Affirmed by the Church of the Savior in Washington D.C., Rev. Gordon Crosby awakened the old memories of spirituality. His prophetic voice stands outside the traditional church, speaking liberation for women, black, and the poor. A liberating voice steeped in the classical disciplines of silence and prayer.

I tried to keep one foot in the church, but my non-traditional approach threatened the very structure, which once was life to me, and then became a place that inflicted pain. Most religious institutions are a place of idolatry: hymns to the father, the exclusion of biblical women in sermons and teachings, the sexist language, and most of all the complacency of my sisters and brothers who say, "We just rise above it, why can't you?"

At this point, deep in my psyche, came the awareness to change my life path that was holding me captive to looking outside myself. My belief was that I must work within the system in order to bring change. I thought I could change the religious structure. I have actively pushed the patriarchal churches' structure; I came to know that change would not happen from within.

It was then that I decided my call was to leave church ministry and go for my doctorate in clinical psychology where I would work with the psychological injuries to women living under the glass ceiling of a Father God.

During my changing paths from master's in theology to doctor of psychology, I spent a lot of time in silent retreat, journaling and reflecting on myself.

Along with my spiritual and psychological awakening came my physical awakening. My body holds my feelings and if I don't let her lead, I get sick. My body is alerted far in advance of my conscious awareness that my psyche is in trouble. I continually struggle with my mind being all-powerful. This was revealed to me very pointedly as I was preparing for a body journal seminar. During the meditation, the symbol that emerged for my body was a body encased in a brain like a baby looks curled in the womb. This active imagination jarred me back to taking very intentional time to rest and play. I had become all head.

When a woman doesn't know her feelings, she certainly will not know her body. The world created a homogenized human called "woman." Finally, the sin is up!

In 1985, with much destruction and reconstruction behind, I was at a good place. I was in graduate school, working for my doctorate in psychology.

During my intentional focus on my inner journey to the conscious Self I met other women who were on the same path and were also balancing their inner exploration with their outer journey. These women, I love deeply. Together we marched for equal rights for women, fought against racial inequality, and created housing for troubled teenagers in our community. They are wise women; they are wild women in the womb and the light with me. With these women I can carry the lineage of the Mother God. They helped me to know more fully who I am, and who I can thrust forward to become.

We have woven for each other a garment of prophetic utterances, a girdle of passion, a breastplate of compassion, a sheath of focus, a veil of tears, and a crown of joy. I was home. My new consciousness was finding affirmation in my work, and yet, I find myself searching the landscape for another crossroad. At each point of my life when a road has come to a definite halt there appears another road. The crossroad has always been much more radical than I was ready to choose, but the necessary education or relationship has always been available to help make the transition possible. I believe I am getting ahead of myself and I need to trust the process of myself. I sat in my chair, reflecting on my life's journey, my favorite books piled around me: The Chalice and the Blade. Eisler, R., When God was a Woman. Stone, M., Goddess in Every Woman. Bolen, J.S. to name a few. I was feeling the power of my choices. This chair was one of them. I bought myself a wonderful, plush, winged-back chair. It was a symbolic gesture of claiming my own power. The men in my life, the men in movies or plays always have their own chair, while the women and children humbly took what was left.

4. MAKING WORDS MATTER

Throughout my private practice as a psychologist, I have heard the life stories of many women. Since 1990, I have been listening to their struggles. I heard them whispering their life stories. My story is included in the whispering. I assured them, made it clear to each of them – their WORDS MATTER! Over the years, there are several words that women use to describe their actions as they tell their life stories – "I've been: too selfish, too quiet, and silent."

Women are convinced of the commonly held truth in our culture that listening to her own voice and attending to her own needs is by definition, selfish. Men are allowed to be selfish. Children are allowed to be selfish. Women do not have societal or personal permission to be selfish. Women feel guilt when they put their smallest needs first. As a psychologist, I have yet to hear as many men express guilt about their choices. Women are raised by society to cater to the needs of others and be presentable and pleasing to others. Men identify with and have internalized Father God, so many men, no matter how old, have the power to do life without feeling selfish or guilty!

The Human story for women and men is described by words. And if only men hear they are like God because God is Father, Male, and women never hear the word God, Mother, She, then women get lost in the process of identity development. WORDS MATTER.

For example, I heard a recent newscast that proclaimed 80 percent or more of women feel guilt for having an abortion. "*No!*" I screamed, I have heard the stories over 20 years, when women speak of their abortion they say, "I feel relieved and grateful for the abortion" and then the conversations lead to, "I feel guilty about being selfish – for choosing myself and my own needs."

The absence of a feminine Godhead for women to identify with is their greatest harm and leads them to silence. Silence concerning their own needs and most importantly silence about being sexually harmed, from a touch to full rape. Today, it has been exposed that when a woman finally comes out from her silence about being sexually harmed, men walk away too many times untouched by law. Women far too often are blamed for men raping them. "They were too seductive, their skirts were too short, their pants too tight," etc., etc. Society, still today, first blames the women, which intimidates them into silence.

I see women always seeking greater understanding in order to free their life from whatever is keeping them from giving birth to themselves. When they give birth to themselves, they soar through the clouds delighting in the light that surrounds them.

Tony Wolfe, Jungian analyst, at a lecture she gave in May 1934, and is still true today: "It is a well-known fact that the number of women who come to analysis greatly exceeds the number of men. This can hardly be due solely to woman's deeper interest in psychology or to her greater receptiveness for the psychological problems of the present day." The process of transformation of the woman's personality, brings her nearer to the true laws of her own unconscious nature. Leading her to her own individuality.

Today, women have been more estranged and have deviated further from their real nature than men. They are more silent in dealing with the difficulties of self-realization and the answer can be connected with the absence of a feminine Godhead. The image of God is the supreme symbol of the highest human attributes and of the most far-reaching ideas of the human spirit. How then, can women find herself if her own psychological principle and all its complexities are not objectified in a symbol, as in the case of men?

The symbol of God takes effect in the human being by gradually unfolding meaning, the meaning society has given it, then, in my world it is a sign, not a true symbol. The relationship with the Deity, according to Wolfe, keeps one in continuous contact with all the conscious and unconscious contents, which the Deity symbolically expresses. Since the Reformation, the feminine principle has disappeared from the church, both in its concrete and in its spiritual aspect: through the destruction of images, on the one hand, and the elimination of the concept of Mother God, on the other.

Today, women are awaking from the silence of their own voice, saying out loud, and yelling from the rooftops what they need in order to live fully. But before they can become aware that there is a problem with the balance of giving, they must first feel the disequilibrium that exists in relationships. Then women can become aware of the need to clear out a space for themselves in the center, and the need to risk rearranging relationships so there can be that space. This may mean the severing of harmful relationships in love or work.

Opportunities in today's society have exploded for women. There comes a wakeup call from deep within the soul of the female spirit. An awakening, a knowing, "I am free!"

Then there is a move that seems to be aided by the recognition that cares for one's self is not necessarily detrimental to her life. It means questioning whether care for self means selfishness. Seeking to be good and pleasing to others, women often submerge their needs, and yet it would seem that they do not remain totally inert, but in fact surface in rather manipulative activity. When the dishonesty of a woman's caring is revealed to herself, a woman can be free to claim her own activity and actively participate in decisions of her own life.

Women are aware of the inequalities and discrimination against women that continue to stunt their development – spiritually, sexually, intellectually, and emotionally. Women are no longer satisfied with being a helpmate for the American system of dominance and oppression. Women must speak from the deeper wisdom that is their history, a history that began in a society, going back to 6000 BCE, where the feminine deities reigned, and women were honored for their power and wisdom. It was a time in history when women and men knew how to balance relationships in forming a society where aggression and dominance were not the norm, but partnership prevailed.

Women need to not only shout their stories from the rooftops, but also shout one of the greatest injuries to the psyche of women, God as male is everywhere and women are excluded. The symbols are everywhere, and men literally have no awareness or need to change the word and symbol of God from exclusively male to include God as female.

Today, women are not silent, but they are still ignored. They tell the pastor, priest, rabbi, and music director, to change the hymns, invocations and the prayers to be inclusive. "Brothers All Are We" doesn't work. How long will this continue? How long will we have to continue to say the important speeches written and spoken "about mankind" which are not inclusive of women?

How long do we pledge allegiance to the flag, "One Nation Under God"? The world goes on, and on, and on – ignoring the experiences of women – in science, religion, politics, education, executive round tables where "rules" are put in place and enforced by male-dominated institutions.

Change cannot happen until women and men, together, address the real issues of including women in the word God. When God the most powerful word describes only Man, Mankind, Him, nothing will change for women. WORDS MATTER.

During my 25 years of practice, I have listened to women sharing their life stories reflecting deeply on their personal experiences. I was so touched by their stories. I wanted to understand how and why women were so much more deeply wounded than men. I developed a retreat where women met to share and reflect on their personal experiences. These women were between the ages of 30 and 80 years old – mothers, grandmothers, single, partnered or married, professional women, such as doctors, lawyers, politicians, scientists, and some on non-traditional or non-professional paths. They came from a spectrum of religious denominations, family backgrounds, sexual identities and they had very different stories than men.

The retreats focused on many topics, for this study, the following are key: 1) How the societal concept of the gender of God as exclusively male affected their psychological and spiritual development: 2) How the concept of God as female has affected their psychological and spiritual development currently. The conclusions of this study indicated several important developmental issues for women:

Some women's autonomy and identity development are deeply wounded at preadolescence (11, 12, 13 years of age), not only as a result of societal stereotyping, but as a result of the absence of a female God transitional object, which carries the girl's identity in simultaneous movement with her tremendous body changes. God as a cultural symbol carries the ultimate identity with wisdom, power, and authority. Without gender identity with this symbol, development is misdirected and confusing at best and more commonly halted.

Women are not innately more relational than men, however, they have attached themselves to relationships as a survival need for self-definition.

God as female carries a spiritual and psychological truth for woman that transcends what they have been taught and experienced. This long-awaited connection for women with the divine enables the possibility of identity and autonomy success.

The knowledge that God had once been worshipped as a Great Mother with breasts and hips and blood flow enabled the women in this study to see their own bodies as sacred. This divine-body connection also enabled them to discover greater acceptance of the weight and shape of their bodies; and, even of great importance, an acceptance and empowerment of their aging process.

The conclusions of this study indicated the importance of going deeper and sharing their reflections to change the world, so I sent letters to offices throughout my city asking for attendance to a study, which would be taped and revealed to all.

5. NO LONGER SILENT

Over the years, during retreats, individual sessions, and special groups, women gave permission to tape our discussions. It was important to record these discussions because their words matter. It was also important that the participants knew they would be heard. Each of the questions is listed below followed by the emerging categorized themes. Under each theme are the direct quotations, which capture the essence of the women's experiences.

QUESTION I: "What was/were your earliest experiences of God and how did you relate to that God?"

My concept of God was developed by going to church and Sunday school every Sunday with my family, and I did that all from the time I can remember until I went away to college. It was pretty much forced upon us as children in our family. But I didn't resent it, because it was a social thing; church was a social thing for me.

I didn't think much about what my concept of God was. I knew in my heart that there was a God and I knew that that God was male, and I knew that that God was loving so basically that's it.

**

My earliest concept of God was that of a male, definitely, and I learned that through my denomination, which is Catholic. And the male God was more authoritarian than loving. It's like what God said, I did. And there was no questioning of either what the church said that God said or the God that the church presented to me. I just never questioned that.

**

God could save your soul from hell and also turn His back on you. He was too far away to really know you. I was always trying to figure out how to please this far away God. There were a lot of things that didn't make sense to me.

**

Well, my images are definitely male, but I have warm, wonderful memories of our pastor and church.

**

The God I grew up with was definitely male. The biggest thing I remember was I had to be good. You had to win God's love and approval; it wasn't just given. And, you know, if you weren't good, then bad things happened to you. So, I spent my life thinking everything bad that happened to me was punishment from God.

**

I came from a very traditional background. My father was a Methodist minister. I grew up in the church. I might as well have been born in the basement. And I was the youngest of five children and I did everything I was supposed to, and God was definitely an all-seeing male person, dominating. I mean, I didn't question anything, not outwardly. Inwardly it churned and churned and churned for years. I was afraid to question. I just accepted everything the way it was given to me. But I feel like I'm now becoming spiritual and I'm now being able to have a feeling toward my creator and I'm still deeply searching. But it's taken such a long time, because that male dominance was so strong. And I just was not strong enough to rebel. You just do not question when you're deeply entrenched in the traditional church, or I don't think you do? I wasn't able to.

**

That's an easy one for me. I just grew up in the Methodist church and it was a big old man with long white hair and flowing beard and lived in the clouds somewhere. I guess I mostly felt he was pretty judgmental and punitive. I don't think it was really much more involved than that.

**

I think for me it was a very judgmental man, because the first thing I can remember thinking is I had done something bad, so therefore I was sinful, and I would need to fear death. I was too young to know what was necessary to be "saved" and so therefore I was always in a constant fear of God, who was very masculine and very judgmental and breathed "fire and brimstone," words heard, but as a child I took literally.

This God could quote/unquote, "Save your soul from hell," but he could also, for whatever reason, the biblical stories also say that, turn his back on you. So, it was very difficult, I lived in constant anxiety, never knowing exactly how you stood in the question of hell and damnation versus eternity.

**

Well, my parents were agnostics all the time that I knew them, but my dad had studied to be a minster and had gone to theological school and had given it up after a couple of years to be principal and teacher. And my mother's father was a Baptist minister and so I got all this indirectly; it was very confusing. But there was no doubt about who knew everything and who had to be deferred to; that was fathers and men.

And it was interesting because I did go to a community church just on my own – I've been the one in my family who has always gone to church someplace, and we lived in a little town and so I went where the kids were going and so I learned all the Bible stories and stuff like that. Even though my parents were agnostic, I still got a lot of indirect messages about who was in charge and who was the most important. Father and men.

**

I think in my life – I have fainted twice and both times have been in church. The first time I was 13 and the second time I was about 23. That must tell you something about what was going on with me, you know, the kind of fear or part of me that just couldn't accept it, I think, couldn't accept being there that I didn't even know at the time.

**

I think my first realization of God, was definitely an authoritarian type of figure, Jesus, because he was the first one I read about. There was this man who didn't quite fit a male image. He had long hair and had long white robes and that's how it was presented.

And the more the father figure came. Shortly after that, but not immediately, it was presented in Sunday school. I think the prayers that we even had to recite at home were more towards Jesus. I couldn't put a face, or I didn't really connect with a God other than Jesus for a while, but he didn't quite fit my image of what I thought was male or fatherly at that time. But it did get meshed all together very shortly afterwards. Probably before I went to school.

There weren't any women in positions of leadership in our church. There weren't very many women anywhere in positions that could be role models.

**

Women in the church cooked.

**

And rummage sales. Brought desserts, you know, made the cake and made coffee, and the women had the right to do the rummage sales. They cleaned up in the kitchen.

**

Sunday school teachers. I felt that it was my mother that was the one that got us to church. The message I got was, it was very important to my mother that we went. She played a very, auxiliary or supportive role, but had no real authority.

**

It was late in the eighties when we went to the church in Cherry Valley when I was still married. I was on the parsonage committee and we interviewed the new pastor and his wife, and they made it very clear that the women in the church were to assume a secondary role.

And it was a joke to me, because I knew that the women kept the church together. Just what you are saying, the church was held together by women and without them, it wouldn't be.

**

My earliest memories were of going to church, in this big Catholic church, feeling so little and helpless and misunderstood and not having a place there.

And I can remember going to church and always praying. I prayed the most of any 5-year-old child there ever was and there was just never a place for me there, and these priests were so big and powerful, and the whole thing was overwhelming.

We were made to go to church. My family wasn't spiritual; they were religious. The funny thing was we'd go to church as a family and my father would sit five pews behind the rest of us, so it just never made sense. But it was just all this whole male God thing that I never felt like I was in the in-group. I was on the outside. It was like a club for men.

I can remember like five years ago, four years ago, the last time I went to a Catholic church, I tried to make myself go just so I could say I went, and it happened to be the Sunday they were honoring nine priests. They all were marching in like soldiers. I just had to leave and so I did. I haven't been back since.

**

Well, I also grew up with a male God, an authoritarian figure, like my own father. And I didn't question my father or God. I just took on all those beliefs and was very much into being religious. I also know that I was having a very difficult time saying the Lord's Prayer because it said, "Our Father," and I was struggling with my father and male domination issues.

**

Well, religion was religion and the church, I guess, was my earliest memories. It was super important. That was the message that was very important, we always went to church.

I now have memories of how tremendously boring church was. It was such a bore; it was so hard to be there. It was difficult, but I had to go to church, and I was so bored. And I think I had the double message of lots of judgment, not only judgment from the God but also from other church people. Lots of judgment from this fearful God, and also there was a loving God.

For a child, I couldn't quite get it; there was a lovingness but lots of judgment. My mother used the religion for guilt trips, like "I'm going to tell your Sunday school teacher that you did this," or "I'm going to tell God." So, lots of that heavy, heavy guilt. So that was the picture that I had. Loving, but it was confusing.

**

I guess my first memories were that I was taught that God was a loving God, kind of like a shepherd, real gentle man, but it didn't mesh with my experience of life; so I just thought it was all lies and I would never be a part of that. It was out of my reach.

**

And even though I have this image of God as male and my own father being authoritarian, it was about the time of my mother's death that I was in this process of really beginning to question and wonder what the options would be. So, it's like even though God was male, my mother carried a lot of power in continuing that belief. It was her own fear. I just continued on with my mother's own fear.

**

THE MOTHER GOD RETURNS

I guess my memories were that we had a female minister and while she was up there in the pulpit she still prayed to a male God.

So, I didn't come from a God who was mean, judgmental or authoritarian; it was very free flowing in our household, but it was still very male. I still thought of God as father and that was that.

I was trying to reflect back because our family was nontraditional in religion, because my mother was, came from a background of a spiritualist church and my father was a Catholic who left the church, so he really didn't participate in the traditional church. So, my concept of God was vague in the sense that it was spirituality that surrounded my mom and she tended to be the force in the family, and my grandfather was involved in Native American healing. And then my sister decided to go to the Presbyterian church on the corner and mom sent me. I know I thought in terms of God as male, but I had all this other influence that seemed more cosmic.

**

I'm trying to think way back. I grew up in a very strict Lutheran household. My recollection of God was one of a judge, "shouldn't do this, shouldn't do that." So, I was the good little girl. I said my prayers at night and complied with all the rules. Every night we read from the Bible. I was scared of God.

**

I came from a real Atheist type background. I was always searching and asking the neighborhood kids about God. So, I started going to the Catholic church with the neighborhood kids looking for a way to bail out from the violence at home. I'd go to church and the priest, a man, would hold his hands on my head or something, and prayed with me, and then I'd go home and think, "okay, all this horrible stuff at home will stop," and being so disappointed that this God, this man with great power, hadn't done anything.

So, I felt a lot of anger about God and church, a lot of roaring anger, because I just got comforted at church, but there was no protection or change in my family life.

**

What comes to mind is a little prayer that many people learned:

"Now I lay me down to sleep, I pray the Lord my soul to keep, If I should die before I wake, I pray the Lord my soul to take." I used to add an addendum, "And keep it in Heaven," because I was never sure what He was going to do with it. I thought it was an incomplete prayer. I didn't fully trust God. I thought, you know, you had to make it real specific for God. But it was a He, no question about that.

I was educated in parochial school, but not without questioning. From the very earliest age, I would question the things the nuns were teaching me and I began to wonder where they came from, because it didn't make sense to me that we couldn't go to our neighbors' wedding because they weren't being married in the Catholic church; our perfectly wonderful neighbors.

It didn't make sense to me that people in deep dark Africa who had never had a chance to be baptized Catholic weren't going to get to go to heaven. The whole system seemed kind of screwy to me. So, I was questioning.

But God was definitely male. I would like to add though that I always had been given the message that Mary was incredibly powerful.

**

I grew up in a Catholic neighborhood and a lot of the stuff I heard was, "What? I have to go to confession because I swore?" There were a lot of things that didn't make sense to me.

I believe I've always had a concept of God, I could not grasp the judgmental person, if God was so about love. I'm certain that God was male, because I always heard it. But I don't know how much stress I personally laid on that.

**

I grew up in a conservative religious setting with my family. There are so many different names for it now, fundamentalists. And it was abusive and I'm just beginning reading a book by Leo Booth about when God becomes a drug and that's how it was; it was, you know, nothing I did was ever good enough.

God was male, there's no doubt. There wasn't a picture of God, but there was a picture, this big picture of Jesus, up behind the pulpit, with a light shining on it, and wow, that was the big picture.

Everything done in our church, all the leadership, all the direction, was male, and you know, who is to question that? It didn't even enter my mind.

God was always out there, or up there, in the sky.

I had a Sunday school teacher, in third grade. She did a lot of damage to me. What I recall that she said, I will never forget, "Everyone else is more important than you, I, me." I remember trying to let everyone know that I understood that and that everyone else came first. But when did I come first? Not in my family.

But it wasn't until I was at the Unitarian church that I would begin considering the possibility of femaleness in deity and that did include me.

**

I used to think I just had multiple personalities, but really I think the most multiple was my images of God, because I had a very powerful mother and grandmother, so all that stuff they'd say about God, as male, didn't fit, because the people who had power were women in my home.

**

My first image of God, which I cannot seem to shake, I was raised in a Catholic church, is of a man with the white hair and beard sitting on the cloud.

I never really thought of a female image because I was so busy doing, you know, trying to do what the church was telling me to do. But when everybody's talking and stuff, it made me think of when I was 16. I really wanted a car. I remember going out on the front porch and praying, but I prayed to St. Theresa. I had no idea, I've never really thought of this since, but I have no idea why I picked her: I mean she was my namesake and I remember sitting on this glider on my parent's front porch and praying so hard to her that I heard her speak and I knew I was getting this car.

My aunt called me and asked me if I wanted a mink, or diamond earrings and I finally told her I wanted a car. She talked to my parents, and then sent me $500 and I bought the best Volkswagen on the face of the earth. And it worked.

I never thought of that before, but I was praying to a female. It certainly worked, much more than the God stuff. This guy.

**

This Jesus wasn't like anybody that I knew. Even though I had a father that was a very quiet person, it still didn't mesh. There wasn't anybody, a man, who did the things that God did. I'd see him in pictures with animals and children and being very gentle and speaking very softly and touching. It just wasn't like anyone I knew. I mean it was more mythical or a fantastic cartoon character kind of thing.

**

Girls went for the ride, there were not rituals for girls – boys had bar mitzvah or served at the altar – girls were absent from all the sacred places.

**

And I, too, tried to be like my father. I mean, somehow that would have been pleasing to be more like a boy. I was raised on a farm, so it was real confusing, because the women worked as hard as the men, but there was never the honor, or respect, or value given to them at the same time; so, I know it would have made a difference to have a female God.

**

I decided fairly early on that church isn't where it was at for me. That God was sort of Mother Earth because that's where I got my sense of peace and joy. And so, I would say by the time I was adolescent, my sense of spirituality was connected to that, but I still had no real model of personal power. I still saw men as having more value and power than women.

**

I remember being very resentful that boys could be on the altar, but girls or women couldn't. Women could sew altar cloths and sew the vestments, but they could not be a part of the mysteries of the sacrament.

**

Women could be the Sunday school teachers. I often felt that it was my mother that was the one that got us to church. The message I got was, it seemed to be very important to my mother that we went, more so almost than my father, and yet when she went, she played a very, kind of auxiliary or supportive role, and yet this was very important for us that we were there.

**

I know I was seeking a connection with God. The biblical stories talked about these experiences. And I really hungered for those kinds of spiritual experiences, and yet, within my own time as a child within the church, I never found it. Maybe because they were always happening to men in the Bible.

**

I really felt a connection with something spiritual and yet I had the profound feeling of not fitting. I dreamed about becoming Catholic and being a nun, because it was the only church [in which] I saw a place for women.

**

Women couldn't vote in our church. Women had no say.

**

The closest I can come to that is like something, I think someone said, when we first started, about it was real clear that men were who were important as far as priests or ministers, those in authority. And I grew up with that too, plus, in a family of five women, my father was the only man, but it was really clear that men were more important. And what they said had more value; it had more credibility; it carried more weight... What would it have done for my self-concept if there had been a council of mothers who had not only equal say, but also final say… I think that would have had a profound effect on me growing up.

**

I'm finding out whatever didn't feel right before was probably because it wasn't okay to be a woman.

**

I think for me the main message was women don't matter, because I remember when I was 13 years old, I remember sitting at the kitchen table with something my father was – I don't remember what we were discussing, but he said, "You know, in Jewish families, women aren't important. It's only the men that are important" and he said, "That's the way it is." And that really, it really, really did something to me then and I still have such a vivid memory, and I go back to that quite a bit, and I think, God, what kind of message was that? But it was so true because in my church, women weren't important; and in my community, women weren't important; and in my family, women weren't important. You know, it was an Italian family, and the men were the dominant ones in the family and the women weren't important, and that was my message. A feminine God, that would have been so redeeming for me.

Summary on Question I

Responses to Question I indicated a framework within the church, which placed God as male, and therefore bestowed the power and authority of God unto men. This omission of girls and women out of the power or authority of the sacred suggested a position of unimportance and left the women feeling confused about their personal power and self-identity in the world outside the sacred places of worship. The women were also aware of growing up with the presence of God as "out there." God was male, not female and felt unidentifiable, not relatable. The God, who is male, has now been changed for women to an internalization of God as female therefore profoundly affecting their self-esteem, identity and body connection to a sense of God as "inside". This internalization of Mother God, according to these women, profoundly affected their self-esteem, identity, and body connection.

QUESTION II: "Take me back in time to your adolescent years. Describe how the presence and worship of Mother God would have made a difference in your life."

I think it would have changed my life 180 degrees to even be aware of the feminine aspects of God or a feminine God. As far as relating to my body, my church always taught the body was over here and the spirit was over there and if you were truly spiritual, you weren't interested in your body. And I felt conflicted with that, because I liked my body. I like the way it felt when I touched it and I liked it. I really felt that that was okay, even though the church said it wasn't. But I feel like if I knew what I know now about a feminine God, I would have felt much more affirmed in how I felt about my body and I would have gotten something from a feminine God that I didn't get from my mother. I know Mother God would make up for what my mother never gave me.

So even as a kid, as an adolescent, I think being more of a feminine God would have just brought me to a completely different place and helped me to question more and be more aware of who I am, rather than just taking what the church said I must be; rather than feeling the conflicting feeling that I felt when I wasn't what the church said I should be.

**

I think it would have been really different for me to have a female God. In childhood I hated being a girl. I wanted to be a boy, because I think they knew they had all the power. God was male. And I did, I hated being a girl. So, I had no self-esteem. I don't think I began accepting myself as a woman until I turned 30.

I think if I would have had a feminine God and just the role model of femininity, my life would have been much different. I think I would have felt much better about myself as a girl and as a woman and would have been able to accept what came along with being a woman, instead of just hating myself and wanting to be a boy.

**

Adolescence and confirmation go together for me. Two things stand out in my mind: 1) I started wearing a bra, and 2) I started wearing a garter belt and nylons. As I think about it, they were very confining, constrictive kinds of things to have happened to me. It was the time I started my period. Life was made much more difficult by those changes. It was also signaling the fact that I was moving from childhood to adult woman. My body was changing and taking on the trappings of female in our society.

**

I remember sitting through confirmation Sunday with a bra that kept crawling up, that didn't fit quite right. I was a chubby little child, and I remember just being miserable, feeling not a part of what was going on because I was so physically uncomfortable with my new body.

**

If there were a female God that was equal to a male God, we wouldn't have to learn about our bleeding in a physical education class with everyone laughing . . . our blood would be sacred.

**

I remember my mother loved having babies; she had six all together. She just loved babies — baby kittens, baby dogs, and there was always blood and pregnant things everywhere in our house, and I just thought she was disgusting. And when I started developing breasts and started menstruating, I thought, "Now, I'm going to be like her" and I just could not accept it. There was nothing else that connected me to my "mother self."

**

Bleeding would be something that I would be so embarrassed about that I would sit and cry in the middle of class because I was so upset by what was, you know, my body's functions. This would be a celebration time. This would be a time of coming into my own.

**

I mean, I got my menses and did not know anything about it, had not been told, thought I was going to die, that there was something wrong with me, but was afraid to tell anyone. So, it wasn't celebrated, it wasn't anything; it was just something that happened. And I was treated very matter-of-factly when my mother did know.

**

And then the period came and I'm like, "Oh, God, could life get any worse?" You don't have the right to talk about something that most of the world isn't interested in, and men aren't.

**

I remember confirmation, I bought a dress, it was a straight dress and my mother's first comment to me was, "Oh, you're going to have to wear a girdle." That made me feel like there was something wrong with my body all of a sudden, I have to hide it, you know, I can't show these curves.

**

Church made it clear that sexuality of any kind was sinful, and here I am blooming and oozing sexuality with my body for everyone to see. I just wanted to hide my body.

It's at the point where we start looking like women that women stop eating and get anorexic. It's real confusing then, because you don't really look like a woman, you don't really look like a child, and you don't really look like a man. And this is the terrible identity crisis for adolescent girls. They are forced by their body changes to leave childhood and enter a place that is not welcomed.

**

As I began to develop in my sexuality and my body was changing, I am aware that the only female image that the church gave me was the Virgin Mary. How can you relate to the Virgin Mary, who supposedly didn't even have a flow?

Through my physical transition to becoming more female, all of a sudden, I was untouchable by my father; and I didn't get closer to my mother. It was kind of like she didn't know either. It was sort-of like, "you're on your own."

**

I remember hating my body – and staying real thin. While the guys are pumping their bodies up and making them more visible and boasting about their sexuality, I'm hiding.

**

A thought just came to me and I haven't thought of this for years. But I never liked wearing pants underneath my shorts, never, from the time I can remember when I was adolescent, even now. I like the feeling of the wind up my crotch. I really thought that was wonderful. So, I had a fairly good feeling about my body. My mother was very emotionally absent from me. I had to raise myself. I needed something greater than me to wrap Her arms around me. Yeah, that would have been . . . (tears).

**

I remember feeling like I was searching for something. I had no idea what I was looking for; but I do know I grew up with a profound sense of shame about my body, and that I think if there had been a matching female deity I would have grown up feeling more of a sense of at least okay-ness.

Through my physical transition to becoming more an adolescent female all of a sudden I was untouchable by my father, like I was not allowed to snuggle on his lap on the couch; and I didn't get closer to my mother either, it was sort of like, "You are on your own."

It is at that point when me and my friends start looking like women that so many of my friends stopped eating and became anorexic. It is really confusing then, you don't really look like a woman, you don't really look like a child, and you don't look like a man. And this is the terrible identity crisis for us girls. We are forced by our body changes to leave childhood and enter a place that is not welcoming.

**

I remember my father would take from his dresser a slide to show his men friends when they'd come over. It was a woman with large breasts. Mom would get really upset. So, what is the message that I'm getting here? Mother gets upset; father shows all the guys, and it's happening to me. I'm not supposed to be sexual, sensual, or to be voluptuous.

**

I think that probably one of the things that is most sad about that time is that my mother bought into this patriarchal society, the male

God and all of those images that went with it. She was kind of the handmaiden of the patriarch. She was the one that gave voice to those – to actually taking away choices in the name of, "You can't do that because you're a girl," and, "If we have any money to spare, your brothers are the ones that need to go to college."

**

I know when I think about it, it feels like life would have been much more exciting, many more doors would have opened than they did. Because I know the door I went into was, "Be attractive and get your power through the men you're with." I remember picking that door, because I was really a tomboy growing up, and so I remember choosing to be more feminine and go the route of getting boyfriends and being popular and I found out, "Hey, I can do that." But I'm sure that I would have thought about more opportunities, other opportunities besides men as the vehicle for what I wanted to do.

**

I never heard the words from my mother, "You can make it happen for yourself." If I knew God were a woman and the ultimate creator of life, I would have known that I could make it happen for myself. Instead, I just stood there in limbo with nobody to turn to.

**

I wasn't a tomboy, but I could beat up all my boy cousins. I could outrun them. I was bigger and stronger and all of a sudden, I couldn't roughhouse with them anymore. My body changes made me different. I wasn't connected to myself anymore. Who am I?

**

My adolescence was — I was, as I have been most of my life, sort of unconscious. I mean, I was very popular because I fulfilled the role of cute young woman. I had very steady boyfriends all along, and I was a real good athlete, swimmer, and so I fulfilled that expectation of my parents, because I was good at sports. I wasn't so good in academics. I feel that if there had been any feminine part in the God concept when I was growing up... I can't imagine how it could have impacted me.

**

If any part of God were female, society would be totally different, so it's sort of hard to separate all of that, because we would have been validated from everywhere. And I didn't find any validation, even though everyone said, "You're good at this," and "You're pretty," I didn't ever feel like that. Never, ever, inside of myself. I mean, to have a sense of being important, of just being, of wanting to be a woman. I guess I have one more little thing, a big thing actually, to me. I think I might have been able to see that women, or I, as a woman, could be responsible for myself. Not, somebody else was going to take care of me or be responsible for me. How horrible! Jeez!

**

If there had been the female image of God, it would have been like there was someone there, the big presence; especially as far as my body image goes. There would have been a symbol of a voluptuous woman that said, "This is okay, you're like me." There would have been something to cling to, but to not have anything, to be flipped off the earth, left floundering with nothing to hold on to. You have your mother who has nothing either, and never hopes to, there's just nothing there. There is nothing. It's really sad. It's really lonely.

**

If I would have had that, it would have been different. There would have been some connectiveness. I would have been able to trust women more. I would have been able to be nurtured by women. I wouldn't have been in so many disastrous relationships with men that hurt me in every way possible, because I was so needy. I would have said "no" and not kept silent.

**

It's like I kept wanting more during worship, and I know if I had the solid ground of Mother God to stand on, I could just make my leap. I would have been in ecstasy, you know, but the ground wasn't solid. It was more like I'd get ready to make my leap and it would give, like a bog or a mini-tramp or something.

Summary on Question II

Question II provoked the women in this study to remember that adolescence was a time of abandonment by mother, father, church, and society.

At a time when her body was making radical developmental changes, from identity as a girl to identity as a woman, there was no one there. The women experienced adolescence as a time of shame, embarrassment, and constriction. The women agreed unanimously that their own mothers could not bridge the chasm from girl to woman and that they needed a greater presence, a Mother God with hips, breasts, and blood.

QUESTION III: "What was your process that sparked the awakening, allowing you to finally know the God symbol held both the female as well as the male attributes?"

I can remember reading When God was a Woman *(Merlin Stones) and* The Chalice and the Blade *(Riane Eisler) and I was sure that I was going to be struck dead. It was kind of like reading pornographic literature. The sky would open up and you would be struck dead. But it was an 'a-ha,' this makes perfect sense.*

**

It's empowering. The first time I heard someone mention God as female I was in a women's group. I laugh now thinking how long I didn't know the truth for women.

I couldn't understand why it had been hidden for all these years? It made such sense.

While reading and knowing this is true – I wanted to run around and tell somebody, share it with other women. Yet, I wasn't sure it wasn't a sacrilege, and I'd go to hell. Now, my theology is so different I can't believe I was ever controlled by such beliefs.

**

Tried to enlighten church councils to change creeds and hymns to include women. I always tried to make changes in the correct way by going through the channels. Then when that didn't work, I'd change the gender in my head to include myself. That's it you know. Changing the gender of God to female is to finally be included in the power structure of our culture. It is so exciting. We ran into terrible resistance and anger from other women as well as men. I could not compromise. I could not minimize like many women, who say, "What's the difference? God is God." These women did not understand, God, as female, meant women finally became equal in body, in soul, in reality, in self.

**

My husband was a Pastor and I'd sit in church and listen to his sermons and prayers. One time I counted, and he referred to the deity as male 25 times: Our Father, the fellowship, the brotherhood, etc. I finally divorced him because I couldn't live with his inability to see what I was saying.

**

I felt rage, when in my twenties I became aware of the historical literature about Mother God worship. I could no longer worship in church. It was all so logical. Of course, God was also female. How could this have gone on? It was like someone finally saying the emperor has no clothes.

**

First, I tried to compromise and stay in the church. I'd see God as genderless. The earth, light, goodness. But it didn't work. Once I started reading the archaeological studies that 5,000 years ago God was worshipped as a woman, I could not compromise. I knew that I had to have God back as female for my own sense of self.

I always tried to make changes in a nice way. I still didn't want to-you know, it's only been the last few years that I said, "Fuck you." I'm not going to be nice anymore. If you can't handle it, that's too bad.

But I always felt that, gosh, I had to give people time and I had to give them some room to grow and that sort of thing. And I finally decided that they were abusing me, so forget it.

I started seeing God as genderless and that was a survival technique of my own, to see God as genderless, so that was really hard to give up; it was really hard. And it was only when I came very slowly, I became aware of some goddess literature in my early 20s but didn't really play with it.

Then in my late twenties I began to really have a need to do that as I began doing more self-reflection and looking at eastern spiritual literature where God was centered in the self and then having to see God as a reflection of myself, and that was female and that was really hard.

And I think it's still very hard for me, being after 10 or 13 years, but it was very much, very much, a release. I certainly couldn't have done it by myself. My counselor had to help me with that.

**

Before I read or heard about God as female, my transition point was to start looking at eastern religions where God was genderless and centered in the self. Then having to see God as a reflection of myself was difficult. It has been difficult to really see God as female even though I know it makes sense. I still struggle with prayer, but it was very much a release.

**

I did yoga and I think that that helped me with my body image and being more present to my body. I did meditation and I had a couple of ecstatic experiences in which I felt really loved. When I started the meditation, I didn't have any notion about God being female at all, and then the leader had us imagine, in the meditation, God as female. We were to imagine that all the things we liked about God were female. She was nurturing, taking care of us, being there for us, and accepting us for however we are. It was so wonderful. I knew I had finally found God. I'm 75 years old and I would have had a different life if I had known earlier, but it's not too late.

**

It happened for me, maybe four years ago, when I was in therapy. In a therapy session my therapist said, "Martha, what's the difference between men and women?" I shrugged my shoulders, "Nothing." Then she just kind of shook her head a little bit and looked real sad. She said, "Genitals, right?" I said, "Yeah." More shaking of the head and looking very sad. She said, "Martha, you're missing so much." I knew she knew something that I didn't know. I began the search for myself. I read Merlin Stone's When God Was a Woman *and went crazy. I called all my wonderful women friends who 25 years ago were telling me things I couldn't hear. I'm just realizing that I've never really been in touch with me, with myself, so I'm learning.*

It must have been there all the time, but to me, it was really symbolic that this snake, even though it was kind of dead and disintegrated and everything was there because I almost felt like it was symbolizing my rebirth. You know, I've sort of shed a lot of the old, a lot of my old thinking and old traditions and I'm being reborn into this kind of new inner being, and I felt such a part of everything and I've always felt so apart.

**

The first realization was that I was whatever everybody else wanted me to be, my parents, my husband, and then I started to question what the church had taught me and I got to the point where I needed to get away from the church completely. I needed to get away from my family completely, and I needed to get away from my husband completely. I didn't wear my wedding band for a long time, because I needed to find out who I was outside of all these institutions. And in that process is when I started to find a feminine God. It was the wise old woman image of the feminine

God that really became important for me and I started relating to her. She just filled a lot of places that I needed to have filled, and She came into my dreams and unconscious. I'm at a point where I can't go back to church. I don't belong there, I can't. So, I think, just for me, once I started that process of questioning, it just opened a whole new world for me, and it's been a long process, 10 or 15 years, but it brought me to a place of a feminine God. And the feminine God also includes nature.

**

I took a world religion class and just started learning about the different religions. But it really started sinking in that, how can one belief be completely, totally, right, and saying that everybody else is wrong if they don't believe like they believe. So, through that I started becoming more open, just to take in any concepts that were different than this male God that I'd always had. The other biggest turning point was being in spirituality group and really seeing how God can't be just all male or all female. I think I have more of a balance and it's great. And I think since the group last year, I have just felt stronger. I have felt more connected to myself as a woman. I have felt more connected to other women.

Some time back, a woman seminarian came to preach at my Presbyterian church and she talked about God as feminine. It was quite radical. It took me a long time to accept it. It was a slow, slow breaking down of resistance. I think definitely it's been other women that have introduced it to me, other women confirming it for me, and books, reading books and saying, "Yes, it's coming" and then dreams started coming. It's not something you can do alone. Therapy helped. As I became more aware of myself, my needs, my feelings, my thinking – it all came together.

So, I've been doing a lot of reading about it and I find that you can't really do it all on your own. You need to talk with other people who have common experiences, and that's really hard. So, I don't know, there's just been this awakening, just being aware now of the possibilities that are open to me and just being conscious and knowing that I am responsible for this change. And people say, "Well, you can call God She. It's just a matter of semantics." It isn't that at all, changing all those he's to she's, it's about changing the world.

**

I think if I had a feminine God, that male, Father only, God would not have been up there in the sky. God would have been inside here (indicating her heart). Like it is for men.

**

God would have been within; Mother God would have been inside me.

I've really gotten into yoga and imaging God as female and that is the first time I ever realized that God was in me and God was not "out there."

**

What came in my visualization of God as a woman is: She said, "Have no fear, because I will protect you." And I knew that meant I could protect myself because I was not alone. She is within me, protecting me. She is no longer someone outside of me, someone that I need to get connected with. It's more the knowing in my soul that I am feminine, I'm woman, I'm okay, and Mother God is inside me. And I have the power and the guidance and everything that I need.

**

I have an image now that I visualize and meet with Her regularly, whenever I want to. She is very young and very old at the same time. She's very wise and very dark and very light. She's everything and is wrapped in a blanket. In my visualization, I know that she's very present to me. And when I'm in difficult circumstances, I feel Her inside of me or I imagine Her there and She is there, and all of the old feelings I used to have of being empty are not there any longer. That's so important.

**

I love to read scripture; however, I have to change all the "he's to she's." If I leave the "he's" then God is out there and if I change them to 'she's," God comes inside.

**

The thing that keeps coming back to me with the feminine God is She's a part of me, She's in me. No one can take that awareness away.

**

I got divorced and found I had breast cancer and all the traditional things that had seemed to sustain me before lost all meaning, and I floundered around really for quite a while. Then I did some work with visualization. The retreat leader had me visualize a loving benevolent Spirit who is my own, and I got a real vision of what that Spirit was, and that's when the God force for me went from outside male to inside female. She's older, bigger, fatter, and stronger, and She has blue wings like a blue heron, and She comforts me by wrapping around me. And She's still there when I need Her. In here now. She's female and I feel connected to Her.

**

One of the most powerful experiences for me was creating a worship service where the Goddesses spoke. Each women leader spoke as if she were one of the many ancient Goddesses. I felt like I became the Goddess, actually feeling like the voice and the message was not my own. It was probably one of the most powerful experiences I had in terms of internalizing God.

Summary on Question III

The women in the study expressed that they searched for historical data and started reading and searching – determined to discover the history of the Goddess. Their responses in this section reflect that they did not just experience an "inner awakening"– it was intellectual as well. Their individual studies included information gathered from literature including the study of historical archeological documentation, women's sharing groups and retreats, etc.

They answered Question III with great enthusiasm. The worship of a female God for them was a return to the Self. A time of re-connection to their body, to their power and authority as a person. The introduction to Mother God theology was summarized as a great 'a-ha.' It was finding the truth about themselves as women as divine. Another thread was the internalization of God. This process has taken 10 to 15 years and was not easy even with the sense of knowing this was a truth for them.

QUESTION IV: "How has your body concept been affected by your transition to the worship of a female deity?"

It started with therapy for me. Once I got to accepting myself and my own importance, eventually it worked around to what I would call having more reverence and respect for my own life. I was open to the idea that God was female, and then I felt in my body that God was female. Then I was home. I no longer fought against myself about weight. I'm getting older and my body wrinkles and sags are beautiful.

**

I began reading about politics, power structures, and relationships. I kept failing at relationships, and it just kind of coalesced; it was just like a "boom," and all of a sudden, it was right. I don't know exactly how to explain it, except that it made sense. Now those pieces fit together, now my feelings of frustration, anger, failure, all those things began to make some kind of sense. I had dreams that pointed in that direction. My dreams kept showing me that I had a split between my head and body, between the head worship and who I was as a female. I don't think I totally understood it. It's only as I go on that I saw how prophetic that dream was, as I began to evolve and look at these things, my spirituality and my sexuality came back together.

**

For me, I had to find out that I was feminine in the first place. Growing up in my family with two abusive parents, I really didn't have a balance more toward feminine than masculine; it was like, woo, neither; and so, I guess I was kind of neutral. And when I had my son and nursed him, it felt so powerful. And my husband couldn't do it and it was like "Oh, is this what being a female is like?" Three years later I had a daughter. Childbirth was an opening to myself. I felt so powerful nursing my baby. Then I started going to the Grandmother Moon Ceremonies, and most of the good things that I got were from women, and I started talking to God as Grandmother and thinking more of women and the importance and powerfulness of being a woman. Somehow my female and divine body got connected.

**

Somewhere in between there was a political awakening and a commitment to that and I worked for women's rights and everything, and I remembered, as people were talking, I remember seeing Judy Chicago's exhibit at the Chicago Art Institute. I was in NOW, National Organization for Women, and we had a private showing of it. There were about 60 of us walking around that table and seeing these different representations of women's labia and feeling a real powerful connection with that, feeling the sacred in that, and just kind of awestruck by the fact that someone would bring this out into the light and then sharing that with other women who were there.

The thing that followed the knowledge I gained through the reading and women's consciousness groups was the pain I felt. I had so much pain around my vulnerability and my lack of power in relationships, especially to men, my father and the men in my life that I had to do something. I had to attach/connect to something in order to survive the separation process and it was Mother God who pulled me out of clinging to relationships with men, especially at work. I finally told my manager that one of the vice-presidents of his company had grabbed me, put his hands all over my breasts. It happened two years ago, and I stayed silent. But not now!

**

For me worshipping the Mother God is a reclaiming of something that was also seen as a negative in our culture, my sexuality. By feeling the Mother God inside of me, I can feel my body more powerfully. I'm reclaiming my sexual needs. My sexuality is not attached to being young.

**

I would have liked a Mother God because my image of woman was not connected to a body. My mother encouraged my mind. My mother is a lawyer and the only thing important to her has always been intellectual and analytical. I'm very emotional, so anything about me that's physical or emotional was never reinforced. And so, I would have liked an image that had a body connected to it because it's taken me my whole life to reconnect with my body.

**

My whole body is in so much pain that I cannot stay in a church service. I now know I had to disembody, dissociate from my body to worship. I had to become genderless, then make my God genderless in order to try to worship in church. Father God cannot be internalized. My body rebels with pain when I try. It tells me how far away from my body I had to go, in order to survive this patriarchal church and society. I went to visit my daughter a thousand miles away. It was Easter morning and I couldn't stay in church. My whole body was in pain. All the pastor talked about was Father God and all the hymns were about "Men of God" and "Brothers all are we."

I kept trying to go back to the patriarchal church because I am drawn to the ritual, the music, the community but I remember the pain was so awful. The anger is gone now, now I am left with a violent reaction, wanting to throw up, feeling the discrimination at such a deep visceral level. I can't stay.

It's been a validation. For a long time, I didn't feel in my body. It's been a process to become comfortable with my body and my femininity.

**

I think, up until just a couple years ago, I was always afraid to look at myself and seeing the female breasts and the private part stuff. It was like it was ugly, because feminine was ugly and hurtful. And now it's "this is nice."

**

The turning point for me and my body was when I was on retreat and had to draw an image of God as female on a T-shirt. I created this figure of a woman with a large flowing mane, she had very heavy and thick feet, solidly planted on the ground with stars around her. There it was. I don't know where it came from, but there it was. About two years later I was thumbing through a book of Goddess figures and I saw one identical to the one I drew. She was called "Protective Mother." And that's so much a part of how I identify and what I am in my life. I've felt real comfortable in my own skin. I'm about 15 pounds heavier that I've ever been, and I like how I look.

**

I was in therapy and doing bodywork, which supposedly "the issues are in the tissues." I always had "miserable cramps." The bodywork shattered whatever I was keeping there. All of a sudden, I started talking to my woman within, and she was beautiful. I just kept crying and crying and talking and talking. I realized that I had blamed everything on my woman my whole life. Without a Mother God image to connect with I wouldn't have been able to see myself as feminine. Now I call my artwork "Sacredly Explicit Goddess Art" and that says to me we have to be able to put our bodies out and say, "This is as sacred as a tree, as a rock, as a river. God created this as well."

**

I was thinking about when I was really aware that I was a woman. Everyone's been talking about giving birth and my awareness came when I had a dream about giving birth and I woke up with my stomach distended to the point of seven months pregnant. I realized that even though I had been really pregnant before this – really, this was the first time I felt my body and felt pregnant. That was my awareness of the feminine and that was about the time when I started to write to the feminine in my journal. That was a real in-body, body dream.

**

It's interesting that the images that are coming from the traditions, the goddess traditions, they're so sexual. The pictures are ancient and yet absolutely relative to what women need today, in order for women to know that our body as female is divine. Everything's exposed – pictures of the Mexican Mother God with her vagina spread wide open with the baby's head coming out and breasts and hips celebrated. It's like women's art and literature are just pushing up to make our body the divine.

Summary on Question IV

The women in this study indicated in their answers to Question IV that the most profound awareness was a re-connection with their bodies. The knowledge that God had once been worshipped as a Great Mother with breasts, hips, and blood broke women open to see their own body as sacred. This sacredness of their own bodies positioned women's identity back in their selves.

Women expressed an acceptance of the weight and shape of their bodies, as well as a greater acceptance of their aging process.

As women began to feel the power and authority over their own body, they finally stopped being silent. Anyone who touches our body without permission, his name will be shouted from the rooftops.

QUESTION V: "What Dreams were significant in the empowering and awakening of your self-identity?"

An Introduction to Dreams

Dreams serve the psychological development of all people, men and women, by raising a level of consciousness that mirrors our life as we are living it in the current moment.

Dreams tell a story, our story, the story we need to see, feel, and hear, awakening ourselves to a new conscious way of thinking and seeing what surrounds us on the outside and directs from the inside. Some dream pictures are clear and some are vague. Some are pleasant to think of, others are quite distasteful. Yet, I want you to hold the most important idea, all images are parts of ourselves. We give birth to them out of the physiological, psychological and philosophical stuff of ourselves; dreams are our creations.

I required each woman in the research groups in this study to follow her dreams by keeping a journal and then dialoguing with each dream image. Each image has so much to reveal to you on your path to wellness. Our dreams speak symbolically and they bring exactly the guides we need to follow on our path toward our awakening conscious self. The images are always a surprise, birds, snakes, animals, ancient creatures and until we hold them and have the dialogue. They are like wonderful poetry or great art. The symbols mirror for us psychologically what we need to internalize into our wholeness.

Women are dreaming today, outstanding dream images, which are expressing their spirituality and connection to the divine as female. One of the most important and new to the night dream life of women is the Black Madonna. She is an ancient symbol of the female goddesses speaking today to that very deprived areas of the woman's soul which hungers for the value and hope in the midst for women to claim their warrior power.

As you read the women's dreams that were so intentional and focused on their lives during our research, I hope it will reveal within your own life the "A-ha!" moment needed to search your surround within and without for your true self.

Dreams are part of the backbone of our standing up strong and firm rejoicing in knowing ourselves better. Then, we can make ourselves healthier, wiser and more aware of our own needs first and stand firm without guilt.

**

It was a time in my life when I was really, really angry about a lot of things. But I couldn't put my finger on the reason. I put it on myself for the failed marriage and failed relationships. Obviously, I thought I had done something wrong. The dream that I remember came to me at that terrible time and I saw myself in the dream, reading a book with a picture of The Goddess on the cover. In my dream I started to see the big picture of power issues in my life and who's got power and why and how come, and it just kind of coalesced; it was just like "boom." And all of a sudden, in my dream, I knew I had given up my power, my ideas and my feelings in my relationships.

**

THE MOTHER GOD RETURNS

A dream that came to me during a retreat, I was standing all of a sudden there were two whirlwinds, one was on the top part of me and one was on the bottom part of me, and I suddenly saw the split between my feelings and my thinking and what the world was telling about who I was as a female. It's only now today, as I go on that I saw how prophetic that dream was telling me I must be my whole person.

**

I remember having a dream where I finally met this old woman on the level floor of a house. The house was no longer asymmetrical — it was very symmetrical. It was illuminated, everything about it was illuminated, she was illuminated, and in my dream, I came in and I had a feeling of "Ahhh," a relief and release as I stood next to her looking into the mirror, she looked directly at me, and I knew she could be a guide for me. This woman told me with her eyes that I would have all the strength that I would need at this time in my life.

**

I am not very visual, so I don't have dreams that are in 3-D and in living color, but in my dreams, I have deep feelings. When I woke up, I definitely felt like I had someone behind me that I was resting on, who was very substantial and strong. I knew I could stay there as long as I wanted and just lean on her and feel the warmth of her. The presence of this person, she feels larger than life, she feels like a huge female, full of substance, mirroring for me a lot of energy and love.

**

This dream came during the week I was studying for my licensing exam and I am scared to death, thinking, "I will not be able to remember all parts of the brain." Then I had this dream:

I am looking through a large glass window and sitting inside a classroom. There are about 50 women and men all dressed in suits. They are all doctors of psychology listening to a lecture. I am overwhelmed with my fear of failure. Out on the sidewalk there is a man holding a large knife. He attacks me – I fight him off and turn, seeing a door. I started running toward the door and its Dr. Mano, the brain neurosurgeon. I worked with him at Rockford Memorial Hospital when I was a chaplain before I left seminary to go for my PsyD in psychology. Standing with him is a tall black woman. Her hair is cornrowed with a beautiful golden scarf. She is holding a baby. She hands the baby to me. Dr. Mano opens the door and says to me, "I will hold your baby, go and dance with my son." I walk through the door and the music starts. His son takes my arm and leads me to a staircase that leads downstairs – The staircase has many stairs missing. I look at him wide eyes and he says to me, "just leap," so we did and the music plays and when we land – we dance.

**

I had a Black Madonna dream. I was laying on the floor and she was on top of me and she was like midwifing me through something. She was like a therapist. She was straddling me while I laid there. And I was saying, "I won't die, I won't die." She was birthing my body and soul again.

**

Some of my more recent kinds of images or connections with that inner deity have been in the form of a Black Madonna in my dreams. This very powerful, very contained black woman speaks to me sometimes in broken English, pointing to a path I must follow.

**

I had a dream where I was in conflict with all these people running around, and over in the corner of the yard was a large black woman sitting, staring at me. In the midst of all the confusion, she had the sweetest smile on her face and gave me a nod. The dream came several months after I graduated with my Masters, took a new job and finally made my needs known in my relationship. I felt empowered and affirmed by the dream.

**

The dream I had at night that was really powerful was about two years ago. It was of being left in a house at dusk, Jim had forgotten something, and I had left him out there and I went back into the house. It was a deserted two-story white frame house that was near a lake. It was on a peninsula. And I was in there alone and it was getting dark and I went to the cupboard and I took out a cup and I was going to make some tea, but I felt like, "oh, something here is wrong," and I was stirring the cup and my hand was shaking. I could feel in the dream the spoon rattling in the cup. And I went to the back door. It was a screen door and there was an owl and she was on the door and she looked right at me, right in the eyes, and it was the most amazing thing, a white owl. I felt so connected to her. And then, after that, I was looking out, it was dark and there were these hooded men in cloaks and they were beating an owl to death. It wasn't my owl; it was another owl. That was a real powerful dream about my own struggle of believing in my own wisdom.

**

I had a dream that symbolizes still my struggle living in this culture to internalize the female God. The dream: I had my arms around this person, I had my arms around her like a shawl and I couldn't see at first in the dream what it was and then there was light, and it opened, and I had my arms around this feminine Goddess. I have a statue, it's from 2000 BCE, Greece. Her head is formed with hair, and She has huge breasts. The figure was larger than life and I was holding it and then I opened up my eyes and it was the statue. It felt like it was a person, but it was the statue and it wasn't alive. I know now that I embrace the feminine God, but it's not easy in this culture.

**

I had this dream, going back two years, I participated in a meditation group and one particular meditation brought the image of my spirit guide as a Native American, very tall broad-shouldered male chief. At a later time, the image kept merging with this wonderful woman with this long flowing hair, and I kept saying, "No, no, that's not right. It's a male." I always fight with my images. And then suddenly it was complete, it was a woman, and I felt, "wow, I AM."

**

I had a dream during the time I was going to Mundelein College in Chicago. This was 1983; I was finishing my master's degree in Spirituality, which was started by Matthew Fox. The faculty professors were feminist, radical, nuns who had left the Catholic Church. One of my dreams during that time was the following:

I'm walking down the aisle of a large, grand looking Cathedral to join two of my professors kneeling before the Altar. The three of us knelt at the Altar which is a cement ten-foot long by three-feet wide altar. We light the candles surrounding the Altar and looked up. Across the Altar was the most beautiful snake. It had draped itself the full length of the Altar, its head and tail were hanging over each end. The eyes of the stake were staring straight at us and we knelt before Her. In the dream, I was in ecstasy.

The very next day I took a break from classes and walked along Lake Michigan and looking down there was this two-foot piece of naturally carved wood with the face of the snake, eyes darkened, looking at me, beautifully shaped. I picked it up and 20 years later it is still on my goddess Altar.

**

I had a dream two months ago of a snake and it was wonderful. It was really a great dream, very short. The snake in the dream nurtured me and crawled all over me and I just felt so, not sexual, but I felt very sensuous and so alive. I mean, down my legs and my arms and my breasts. And then the head of the snake came up to my face and looked into my eyes, and I looked into its eyes, and it said, "Open your mouth." And I opened my mouth and its tongue went in my mouth and it was so abrasive, I thought that I'd be all bloody. I mean, her tongue was tiny, but it was like little knives. The abrasive tongue changed into this comforting tongue in my mouth and I woke up. I know what that is. It's important I know. I am hurting myself by not speaking my truth!

**

I think one of the most powerful dreams for me is about a year ago. I had a dream about a snake and I knew that it was female, and I knew she was gorgeous, but I was absolutely terrified of her and pulled myself back and warned another woman to stay away from her. My first thought when I woke up was: "Am I afraid to use my own power and say and do what I must for myself?"

**

This dream must have been there all the time, but to me, it was really symbolic. I dreamt that this snake, even though it was kind of dead and disintegrated and everything, it was there because it was symbolizing my rebirth. You know, I've sort of shed a lot of the old, a lot of my old thinking and old traditions and I'm being reborn into this kind of new inner being, and I felt such a part of everything, and I've always felt so apart. Now, I just feel more a part of myself.

**

During a retreat meditation session, I had a visualization of a heron. Then, this happened to me right after I was walking back to my cabin, I found a dead blue heron on the road. And I felt like a witch, because I picked it up and put it in the trunk of my car and drove home with it, and in the dead of night in my backyard, I got the garden clippers and clipped the wings off and I still have one of the wings in my living room reminding me to fly high and not be afraid, but be as graceful as the heron when she stands in or flies just above the water.

Summary on Question V

Question V illustrates the images and symbols necessary to pull women into the future. The Black Madonna, symbolizing the feminine consciousness, and self-power that has been silenced. She mirrors for women our Goddess within, bringing our sexuality and power of God to women. The Black Madonna symbolizes the power, the wisdom, and the self-authority that is hidden from us in the world. She comes bringing light to our darkness within, in order for women to know they are all powerful. She tells us "Be Not Afraid."

The snake is an ancient symbol of transformation and female cycles. The snake, an ancient symbol of the divine, discovered in archaeological studies of Mother God temples of worship, is returning to re-connect women to their divine self.

Native American figures, animals, and birds bring the matter and spirit connection of the divine. Women need new images and symbols with which to express their spirituality and connection to the divine. As women connect to the Divine as female they are completing the autonomy and identity work that was left undone.

Birds wrap their winged arms around us, circling us protectively, while raising us up, encouraging us to fly and see ourselves in all of our fullness and power.

6. REFLECTIONS ON THE WOMEN'S STORIES

The findings of this study indicate that religious discrimination has made a most profound mark on the psychological development of women. I believe there is major evidence in the stories and experiences of women – that growing up in a patriarchal culture and society, which identifies God as only male, with ultimate authority – has detrimental effects on women's psychological development. This power and authority of a male God has been placed by society, on men in our culture. Women have had to subjugate themselves not only to a male God but to men in general. This has left women connecting to men and a patriarchal structure in order to have some of this power and authority for themselves. They also reflected how their silence of sexual abuse in work areas was due to fear of losing their job. Many workplaces had no policy in place to deal with these situations. If the woman did report such an incident, her words were not given equal authority of the truth over men's, she became abused by management and their unwillingness to deal with the abuser. This furthered the pain and assured silence in other women.

Though many of the women who told their stories are educated, professional, economically stable, and politically active, they still had identity, self-esteem, and body image issues, as well as feelings of not being connected to Self and being overly connected to relationships. When these women discovered through consciousness raising groups, psychological therapy sessions, friends, world religion classes, and reading that the ultimate authority in society, God, could also be female, there was a process of shifting power from "out there" male to "inside personal" female. Therefore, women stated: "If God has authority and power, and God is female, then women have power and authority innately."

For these women the Father God out there radically moved to the Mother God inside themselves. This internalization of God as female, according to these women, profoundly affected their self-esteem, identity, and body image.

This newfound knowledge turned women's lives upside down. The most profound awareness was a re-connection with their body. The knowledge that God had once been worshipped as a Great Mother with breasts, and hips, and blood, broke them open to see their own bodies as sacred.

First, they expressed an acceptance of the weight and shape of their bodies, and, most importantly, an acceptance and honoring of their aging process.

Second, this sacredness of their own bodies positioned their identity back into their deeper Self. These women had long ago learned to mistrust their bodies and emotions, thereby mistrusting their own experiences. This alienation from the very essence of her being distances a woman from her center.

Third, and very importantly, women took control of their bodies – they were now the power and authority over who and what could touch their body.

In light of the women's movement of liberation and spurred on by a deep gnawing ache from emptiness, women are questioning traditional notions regarding religious authority, divinity, and liturgy, and are now challenging old models and demanding new understandings of history and theology. Women are reassessing and redefining who they are as spiritual beings. Women are now reclaiming connection with – and awareness of – their bodies, its functions, its sensuality, and sexuality. Rather than existing in the dualism that splits body from soul, women are seeing their bodies as paradigms of feminine identity. In other words, women access spirituality, hence, Mother God, through awareness and appreciation of their bodies. Today, with the power of Mother God, they are saying NO to men who think they can feel a woman's body without permission.

The primary religious symbol in ancient times was that of a woman giving birth. How well the ancients knew of the essence of God as Mother. Aspects of the female body that allow women to understand the cyclic flowing of life-giving and life-sustaining blood, the dark, mysterious water-filled womb that begets, gives form to, and brings forth new life.

7. CALL FOR CHANGE

The audacity of excluding women from the Godhead and the outrageous arrogance of excluding women from the symbol of God. It is unbelievable that we have lived our lives not being seen. It is as if there is only one species, Men, one God, Father and one authority: MAN.

As I awakened into consciousness, I looked at my body and thought, "Wow, where have I been all these years?" No mirror of the most high to reflect ME. Humans do not truly honor the female.

Women, close your eyes, take a breath and reflect on our world, thinking how men could have been so arrogant to create God as male. Leaving out all female images and words for the most powerful object of authority in the world: God. Creator of all. The pastors, rabbis, and priests say to women, "You are born in God's image." Let's see, God is Father, Son, Man, and we are Mother, Daughter, and Woman! We are not born in the God image in the world today. Today's God is male. In order for women to be born in God's image, God must be Female, Mother, Daughter, and Holy Spirit as well.

For years men have defined the identity of God as male. What have been the results of only a male, Father – God, in the psychological development of women? Silence… only silence. They tried but then they were hung, drowned, and burned to death as witches. Brute force, masculine strength, and violence stopped women's voices. That force silenced women and continues yet today, years later. It's over. Women are slowly and deeply feeling the emptiness of the absence of Mother God in the world.

Powerful men have erased our history and the women today have awakened from a long sleep questioning, "Where is our God? Why isn't She deep within us? Why isn't She holding us in our pain and leading us in our unfolding lives?"

It is beyond reason to think the world of women has been lost to themselves. No Mother God to identify with, to mirror our bodies, to hold us up to reach for the sky in order to be all we are born to be. We have been silenced and now we must engage and call out Her name, demanding change. Call out Her name, Mother God, Goddess, She, Spirit Woman. Change begins with each of us standing proud in our bodies, in all its imperfections, and calling out for Her to guide us, support us, love us, and mirror to us, as She walks the path with Him.

APPENDIX

Biographical information on group participants

There were four groups of women, a total of 30 in all. Each group contained women between the age of 30 and 75 years from a spectrum of religious denominations. There were 24 heterosexual women and six lesbians. Of these, 15 women were married (including committed lesbian relationships), 16 were divorced, and six were remarried. A total of 24 women had children; six had no children.

Some of the professions that were represented in the research include: marketer, massage therapist, program coordinator, homemaker, nurse, counselor, administrator, and educator.

Group 1

41 years, divorced, one child, associate degree, respiratory therapist, nondenominational Christian

59 years, married 35 years, three children, master's degree in education, school counselor, Presbyterian

38 years, married, one child, two stepchildren, three years college, temporary worker in marketing, United Presbyterian

49 years, divorced, three children, master's degree in maternal child nursing, certified OB-GYN nurse, program coordinator of women's program, Lutheran

51 years, divorced, three children, master's degree in business, Catholic

75 years, widowed 20 years, three children, licensed clinical social worker in private practice, Baptist/agnostic

34 years, married 13 years, two children, bachelor's degree in nursing, Catholic

Group 2

47 years, married, one child, master's degree in education, special education department administrator and teacher of behavior disorders at middle school, Missouri Synod Lutheran

46 years, single, master's degree in education, Department of Children and Family Services, Catholic

39 years, married, two children, bachelor's degree, nondenominational Christian

52 years, married, six children, post-doctoral fellowship in spirituality and psychiatry, Catholic

43 years, single, lesbian, artist, nondenominational Christian

54 years, divorced, three children, bachelor's degree in nursing, addictions counselor, Mission Covenant Church

46 years, divorced and remarried, one child, LMSW, school counselor, nondenominational Christian

37 years, married, lesbian, one child, bachelor's degree in English, AIDS counselor, Catholic

46 years, married, two children, high school graduate, works in home, Lutheran

---

Group 3

40 years, married, lesbian, master's degree in education, physical education teacher, Catholic

62 years, divorced, three children, high school graduate, receptionist, Lutheran

30 years, married, lesbian, master's degree in art therapy, art therapist, Catholic

40 years, divorced and remarried, four children, master's degree in spirituality, private practice psychotherapist, small fundamentalist Christian church

39 years, married, two children, master's degree in art therapy, private practice art therapist, Congregational

41 years, divorced, three children, lesbian, Missouri Synod Lutheran

39 years, single, lesbian, no children, bachelor's degree in communications, public relations, Methodist

---

Group 4

46 years, divorced and remarried, one child, master's degree in social work, Counselor Community Mental Health Clinic, Presbyterian

61 years, divorced and remarried, one child, high school graduate, homemaker, Methodist

49 years, divorced and remarried, two children, bachelor's degree in English literature, certified paralegal, Congregationalist

40 years, married, no children, master's degree in pastoral counseling in progress, hospital chaplain, Catholic

40 years, single, lesbian, no children, bachelor's degree in human resources, mental health counselor, fundamentalist Christian church

47 years, divorced, lesbian, two children, bachelor's degree in nursing in progress, massage therapist, nurse, Lutheran

49 years, married, three children, LMSW, private practice psychotherapist, Missouri Synod Lutheran

BIBLIOGRAPHY

Avery, C. S. (1991, November). Voyage to womanhood. *New Woman*, 58-66.

Bolen, J.S. (1984). *Goddesses in Every Woman: A New Psychology of Women*. Harper & Row.

Campbell, J. (1972). *Myths to Live By*. Bantam Books.

Einsler, R. (1987). *The Chalice and The Blade*. Harper & Row.

Gimbutas, M. (1989). *The Language of the Goddess*. Thames & Hudson.

Kaschak, E. (1988). Limits and boundaries toward a complex psychology of women. *Women & Therapy*, 7 (4), 109-123.

Kaschak, E. (1991). *Engendered Lives: A New Psychology of Women's Experience*. Basic Books.

May, R. & Yalom, I. (1989). Existential Psychotherapy. In R. Corsini & D. Wedding (Eds.), *Current Psychotherapies* (pp. 363-404).

McDargh, J. (1983). *Psychoanalytic Object Relations Theory and The Study of Religion: On Faith and the Imaging of God*. Univ. Press of America, Inc.

Pinkola Estés, C. (1992). *Women Who Run with the Wolves*. Ballantine Books.

Rizzuto, A. (1979). *The Birth of the Living God: A Psychoanalytical Study*. Univ. of Chicago Press.

Silverstein, S. (1964). *The Giving Tree*. Harper & Row.

Winnicott, D.W. (1971). *Playing and Reality*. Tavistock.

Wolff, T. (1934). *A few thoughts on the process of individuation in women* (Report). Psychological Club, Zurich.

ABOUT THE AUTHOR

Renee McArdle, PsyD, is a licensed clinical psychologist, a spiritual teacher, and social justice activist dedicated to the evolution of consciousness for all people. She has been a psychologist in private practice for more than 25 years, a hospital chaplain, co-founder of Common Boundary Wellness Center, and Manitoumi Retreat Center. Over the years, she has led therapy groups and retreats using myths and silence to expand conscious living. In her private practice, she uses dream analysis, hypnosis, guided imagery, and unconditional acceptance. Renee continues to be dedicated to changing the language that excludes women in the organized churches. Her research supports her belief that the exclusionary language in the church has diluted the potency of women's identity psychologically and in the world! Her Irish and Welsh roots drive her Celtic mind to believe in the "invisible world" and the mystery that surrounds us all! We are in the home stretch of our lives, spirituality, and science.

Made in USA
Fair Andreen, Inc.
W238 N1650 Rockwood Drive
Waukesha, Wisconsin 53188
979-8-89504-135-2